This I Know

Tracey Davenport

Parson's Porch Books

This I Know
ISBN: Softcover 978-1-955581-66-0
Copyright © 2016 by Tracey Davenport

To order additional copies of this book, contact:

Parson's Porch Books
1-423-310-8815
www.parsonsporch.com

Parson's Porch Books is an imprint of Parson's Porch & Company (PP&C) in Cleveland, Tennessee. PP&C is an innovative company which supports people who live in poverty by allowing them to earn money by assisting in publishing books by noted authors, representing all genres. To help people in poverty, PP&C totaling depends on the generosity of its authors and partners.

This I Know

Table of Contents

These sermons were meant to be heard, not read. My sincere prayer is that everyone who reads them senses the love and passion with which they were proclaimed in worship. As you read, may the Spirit of God convince you of God's great love for you in Christ Jesus our Lord.

This book is dedicated to the congregations

which have endured my preaching,

encouraged my gifts and

loved me like Jesus loves me.

Philippians 1:3,

Tracey

Talking with Moses and Elijah

Mark 9:2-9

I have a friend who is dying – she probably has a few weeks left. I love her. I enjoy her company. And the dreaded clock is ticking away, sand running out in the hourglass of her time on earth, and I cry every time I leave her for I fear it may be the last time. Time for me is a constant constraint. There are never enough hours in the day to do what I want and need to do. There are never enough moments with the people I love. And the older I get, time seems to get faster every year. Have you ever had a day you thought would never end? And have you ever had a day you wished would never end? I have, but they always do, and I am back to world again.

I believe Jesus felt that time urgency when he was on earth. I believe he loved his disciples and enjoyed his time with them. I believe time moved very quickly through his three years of ministry. He had to get to all to the towns in the Galilee. He had to make his way to Jerusalem. The storms of resistance and hatred toward him by the religious leaders only intensified that feeling.

And so, six days after he tells his disciples that he must suffer and die, six days after he says, "Truly I tell you, there are some standing here who will not taste death until they see that the kingdom of God has come with power," Jesus takes Peter, James, and John, his closest friends, up the mountain. Once they get there, something very strange happens: Jesus changes. His clothes become dazzling white, and he is seen talking with Moses and Elijah. Moses, who met the Most High God speaking to him from a burning bush that was not consumed, who led God's people out of slavery in Egypt, who gave them the Law of God and took them to the edge of the Promised Land, is standing there talking with Jesus. Elijah, the great prophet of old, the one who stood up to the corrupt King Ahab and Queen Jezebel, the one who heard God's still small voice on a mountain, the one who did not die, but was carried into heaven by a whirlwind, is standing there talking with Jesus. For just a moment, the boundary between time and eternity is transgressed. Time is neither a barrier to their relationship nor an urgent constraint. They seem on this mountain to be outside of time. It is a terrifying moment – Jesus suddenly changed, history suddenly visible, the voice of God speaking. It is so terrifying Peter starts talking nonsense about having to build shelters for each of them. And then, before they know it, it's over. Moses and Elijah disappear. Jesus becomes again who they are used to seeing. Eternity backs out of our time once more, and they head back down the mountain.

Biblical scholars call this passage the epicenter of Mark's gospel, the watershed moment. We knew we were heading to something big from chapter 8. Jesus asks his disciples who he is and Peter gets it right: "You are the Christ, the Messiah," he exclaims. Jesus confirms Peter's answer and then explains what that means. It means he must suffer and die and after three days rise again. The tension mounts. What will happen next? Soon after, Jesus invites his three closest disciples to witness something incredible.

Who is Jesus? That's the question and Mark's gospel is giving us pieces of the puzzle. He is the One with authority. He is our healing Savior. He is our Friend. And today, from this passage, we see that Jesus is eternal. Jesus is the One Eternal God. From John's gospel, we hear Jesus claim, "Very truly I tell you, before Abraham was, I am." This is a very clear claim to be the One Eternal God.

What does it mean to be eternal, to be without the limits of time? Economist E. F. Schumacher liked to tell a joke about it. One day a philosopher out walking in the woods came face to face with a figure in a radiant beam of light - none other than God himself. As he had spent a lifetime pondering God's existence, the philosopher was awed, but only temporarily.

"You are the Lord, I presume." "Yes," said God, "I am." "Well then, my Lord, I wonder if you would be good enough to answer a few simple questions that have been troubling me for some time." "Certainly, my son." "Is it true, Almighty, that what is for us a million years here on earth is for you nothing but the merest moment?" "Yes, my son, quite true." "And is it also true," the philosopher went on, "that a million dollars here on earth is for you nothing but a paltry penny?" "Also quite true."

The philosopher paused only a moment. "Then, I wonder if it would be possible for you, if it is not too much trouble, to give me a penny?" "Why, certainly, my son," said God. "I'll be back in just a moment."[1]

The Psalmist proclaims that a thousand years is like just a watch in the night for the God who is from everlasting to everlasting. Theologian Karl Barth called the eternity of God one of God's "perfections." "Time is a creation of the eternal God. Time has no power over God. As the eternal One, it is he who surrounds our time and rules it with all that it contains. God is personally present at every point in our time. And the fact that the Word became flesh undoubtedly means that, without ceasing to be eternity, in its very power as eternity, eternity became time. In Jesus Christ, God takes time to himself and becomes temporal. If this is so, we cannot understand God's eternity as pure timelessness. True eternity has the possibility, the potentiality of time."

---

[1] Homileticsonline.com

Barth continues: "God is therefore, in his eternity, the master of time. He re-creates it and heals its wounds, lovingly redeeming the fleetingness of the present and the separation of the past and future from one another. God becomes one of us in Jesus Christ so that our time, with its defects, is not so alien to him that he cannot take it to Himself in his grace, mercy, and patience, himself rectifying and healing it and lifting it up to the time of eternal life."[2]

Believing and trusting the God who is eternal, what difference does that make? Following God, who was eternal enough to become temporal in Jesus Christ, what could that mean for this life and the life to come? What's the big deal, besides the novelty of it, of seeing Jesus in his dazzling eternal state talking with Moses and Elijah?

Maybe it means time is less important than I think it is. Maybe all time is in God's hands and my striving and urgency work against God's good plan. A British father wrote that when he was on an outing with his family, his wife implored their daughter Molly to hurry up because there was "no time to stop and blow dandelions." In response, Molly raised what may be for a child - perhaps for all of us - a major philosophical and spiritual issue. "Mummy," she said, "what is time for?"[3]   Is it for blowing dandelions and being with those you love and growing in our relationship with God and with each other? Can I relax and do the things I am called to do and not worry about time to do the rest? Can I let the God over all time heal its wounds and bring forth his amazing plans? Can I place my friend who is running out of time in the hands of the One who is eternal?

---

[2] Karl Barth, *Church Dogmatics*, Vol. II (Edinburgh: T & T Clark, 1957) 608-640.

[3] John L. Locke, *The De-Voicing of Society: Why We Don't Talk to Each Other Anymore* (New York: Simon & Schuster, 1998), 172.

But maybe this means time is more important than I think it is. We are each given an appointed number of days on this earth by the eternal God. Should we not make the most of them? You have heard the following: To realize the value of one year, ask a student who failed a grade. To realize the value of one month, ask a mother who gave birth to a premature baby. To realize the value of one hour, ask the lovers who are waiting to meet. To realize the value of one minute, ask a person who missed the train. To realize the value of one second, ask a person who just avoided an accident. To realize the value of one millisecond, ask the person who won a silver medal in the Olympics. Does this not teach us to value each moment we are given?

The Psalmist writes: "Teach us to count our days that we may gain a wise heart (Psalm 90:12 NRSV). And likewise, Paul writes to the Ephesians: "Be careful then how you live, not as unwise people but as wise, making the most of the time, "(Ephesians 5:15-16 NRSV). How much time do we spend doing things that matter, that are of value, that make a difference in the world? We are not given any guarantees by God about time. What might we do if we knew we have just one week left? Would we gather with those we love? Would we pay off debts? Would we ask for forgiveness and make amends? Would we share our testimony with someone else? Would we talk to God more this week?

Occasionally, when we humans can at the same time give up our obsessive control of time while realizing its true importance, we come upon a time that seems to transcend time and take us into eternity, if only for a moment. "Really?" you ask, "because it has been a very long time since someone claims to have seen a burning bush that was not consumed, or the chariots of heaven and a friend taken up in a whirlwind, or Jesus with Moses and Elijah chatting it up." Granted, but remember these things are often kept a secret, because they can be terrifying and wonderful, too wonderful for words, until time has passed and it is safe to share them. I will share one with you.

I was sitting in Starbucks this week. So many spiritual things happen to me at Starbucks! Maybe it's the caffeine. Anyway, for months now I have been asking God for something. On Wednesday afternoon as I was enjoying my tall, skinny hazelnut latte and composing this sermon, I heard the familiar ding that an email had been received. I almost didn't check it, but I decided to. It was the news that was the answer to my prayers. Tears streamed down my face, my spirit crying "Thank you! Thank you!" to God. The outside world faded away and I found myself in the presence of the Eternal God. I don't know how long I was there – I did not look at the clock, but it was as if time did not have a say in the matter. I stayed there a while, saying thank you, hearing the words of one of my favorite Isaac Watts hymns: *My Shepherd will supply my need; Jehovah is his name. In pastures fresh He makes me feed, beside the living stream. The sure provisions of my God attend me all my days, O may Your house be my abode, and all my work be praise.* Did I just space out or was the boundary between time and eternity not so thick at that moment?

Eventually the sound of the hymn disappeared and the noise of Starbucks returned. Eventually I got back to my schedule: a sermon to be written; a child to be picked up from school; shelter guests to be transported to our church; dinner to be made. But what stayed with me is that my time is in the hands of the One Eternal God – who is not constrained at all by earthy time. My time is redeemed by Jesus, the eternal God made flesh and dwelling in our time. So, the next time I feel like the demands of time are overwhelming me, I will picture Jesus in my mind, dazzling white, talking with Moses and Elijah, and I will trust the One Eternal God with all my time.

Ask, Seek, Knock

Luke 11:1-13

Jesus is teaching his disciples how to pray in response to their request to learn. Specifically, he is teaching them about prayers of petition, prayers of asking God for something. Petitionary prayers are found all throughout Scripture. Moses, David, Kings of Judah and Israel brought their requests to God. Paul reports pleading with God to remove the thorn in his flesh. The early church prayed fervently for Peter when he was arrested and thrown in jail. All of God's people engaged in prayers of asking God for what they needed or wanted. Jesus petitioned God to heal people, to open blind eyes, to protect his disciples. Jesus prayed, "O Lord, let this cup pass from me." Jesus asked his Father to forgive those who crucified him.

So, Jesus sums up his teaching on petition with this command, "Ask, and it will be given you; seek and you will find, knock and the door will be opened for you." This is our part in petitionary prayer and the first important principle of petitionary prayer: **Our command from Jesus himself is to ask, to seek, and to knock.**

Asking here may refer to physical and material needs and wants. "Lord, please heal my mother." "Lord, I may not have enough to pay my mortgage payment this month." "Lord, please protect my daughter as she drives by herself back to college." We can and should ask God for help with our physical and material needs. Seeking in Scripture often refers to looking for wisdom. "Lord, guide me as I make this business decision." "O God, help me to be a wise parent." "O Lord, I don't understand why this happened to me." Think of knocking as asking for spiritual help. Luke reports that Jesus often opens spiritual things for people: their eyes, their minds, and the Scriptures. We may pray, "Gracious and forgiving God, help me to forgive my brother." "Jesus, I cannot feel your love for me." "Lord, help me to not give into this temptation one more time."

I have often asked the question, "If God knows what we need and want before we say it, why do we have to ask?" Aren't we telling God something God already knows? Yes, we are. But the asking is not for God, it is for us. Asking helps to clarify what we need and want. Seeking makes us aware of our need before and dependence upon God. Knocking opens dialogue with God. Petitioning God builds our faith because it acknowledges that we believe God has the power to answer and fulfill what we have asked.

In this passage Jesus assures us that God will give in response to our asking, that we will find in response to our seeking, and that the door will be opened in response to our knocking. These are not empty, optimistic words. I believe they are true. But, these words are not a blank check. They do not give us license to ask for anything we can dream up or imagine. This brings us to the second important principle of petitionary prayer. **The command to ask, seek, and knock assumes the petitioner has already prayed the following words from earlier in Jesus instruction: "Father, hallowed be your name. Your kingdom come."** The command to ask, seek, and knock is to those who more than anything are seeking God's kingdom and God's glory. Those who first desire what has eternal significance are told to ask, seek, and knock.

We humans often mix up what is valuable for eternity and what is not. Have you noticed that so many things we have thought we wanted, asked for, fought for, and received have not been good for us in the long run? Humans often miss what is good for God's kingdom and what will bring God glory. We miss what is even good for ourselves. I am not suggesting though that we filter our prayers beforehand. It is in the asking that God reveals to us what is truly needed for God's kingdom and what is not. Righteousness, peace, health, wholeness, justice, compassion, mercy, and faith are just some of the categories of our petitions which have eternal value and significance.

Sometimes our petitions are answered in a different way than we imagined because of God's wisdom and loving plan for our lives. I petitioned God for three long years to adopt a five-year-old from Texas and was given a three-year-old from Kazakhstan. Is it okay with me that God altered and answered my request to fit his plan and not mine? You bet it is. What I received is far better than anything I could have possibly imagined. It is only in looking backwards that we can see just how wonderfully and miraculously God has answered some of our requests. It is only in looking backwards to see how trustworthy God has been, that we can then look forward in faith.

Sometimes our petitions are answered with a no. I can understand many reasons why God would say no to us: God has something better for us; God has set up certain physical laws in the universe that are not to be suspended; God has given all of us free will; God longs to protect us from harm we may not foresee. But, the truth of the matter is, when God has answered me with a no, I have not known the reason. I have prayed for persons to be healed, young people with many more years of life ahead and many gifts to give to the kingdom of God, and they have died. The early church prayed just as fervently for James as they did for Peter, and James was martyred. What if I petition God for something big and it never comes about? What if I pray for healing and the person dies? What does that say about my prayers? What does that say about God? Wouldn't it be better to lower our expectations, to ask for things that cannot be measured, or to ignore the part of this passage where Jesus says, "Everyone who asks receives, everyone who seeks finds, and for everyone who knocks the door will opened"? Jesus in no way models or suggests that we pray with a sense of detachment or with a lack of care for what happens. Jesus never shied away from asking God, even to the point of yelling in pain on the cross, "My God, my God, why have you forsaken me?" Jesus, until the end, was asking, seeking and knocking with passion, just as he commanded us to do.

My chiropractor just adopted a little girl from China, his fourth little girl from China. She badly needs a heart transplant and it is a miracle she made the trip home to the United States. But, last week he found out that her lungs are worse than they thought. She may not get a new heart because she would not survive the surgery. It all depends on a test in two weeks. Chances are slim that she will pass the test. Am I still going to beg God to intervene and help her get the new heart she so desperately needs? Yes, I am, every single day.

This brings me to the third, final and most important principle of petitionary prayer. Our passage today tells us far less about how to pray, than it does about the One to whom we pray. When we don't know anything else, when all our petitions seem to have come back stamped "request denied" we know that God is our Father. **God is a generous father who loves his own and desires to provide for our wants and needs far beyond any earthly father or friend**

One Sunday during worship in San Angelo, Texas Jack was praying. The praise team was singing *I Love You Lord* after the prayer of confession and Jack had his hands in his lap, opened upward. He then brought his hands together, open and held out, just like our three-year-old Alia did when she asked for something. His eyes were closed and suddenly he felt something fall into his hands. He opened his eyes to find one Honey-Nut Cheerio, placed in there from her bag of worship munchies. She had seen his hands, open and asking and so she gave.

Friends in Christ, if a three-year-old sees someone asking for something and gives, how much more will God? If an earthly parent responds with good gifts to their children, how much more will God, who is goodness itself, respond? If an earthly friend will give, even for the wrong reasons, how much more will God, who loves us, meet our needs? If an earthly parent will say no to the harmful request of a child, even at the cost of a temper tantrum and some embarrassment, how much more will God protect those in His tender care?

I believe the most glorious time will be when we get to heaven will be able to ask and seek and knock face-to-face with God. I believe then we will know all the requests God fulfilled that we missed while on earth because they were not what we expected and we will be thankful for such a great Father. I believe we will also know all the reasons that our requests that were denied and be thankful for such a great Father.

What do you want? What do you need? Tell God in prayer this week exactly what it is. Ask for healing. Seek the answer. Knock for forgiveness and love. Trust that in the asking, seeking, and knocking, you will be given the Holy Spirit, the very presence of God in your life, by a Father who loves you more than you can imagine.

Providence

Matthew 6:24-34

This passage of Scripture, right in the middle of the Sermon on the Mount, has been for me one of the most life-changing, most foundational, and most comforting that I have come to know and believe. This teaching of Jesus confirms what we call the doctrine of providence: God's special, personal, and loving care for us and all created things.

Jesus spells it out for us, first, by telling us to look at the birds of the air. It's our heavenly Father who feeds them. Consider the lilies of the field. Even King Solomon was not clothed as gloriously as they. If you have even been in the Texas Hill Country in the spring when the bluebonnets are in bloom, you know Jesus is right. And if God so clothes fields of grass and if God feeds little birds, will God not also care for us, the pinnacle of His creation? Will He not care for you and for me just as thoroughly and just as wonderfully?

Because of Jesus' teaching, we are convinced that "God is personal and that God is personally active in all his creation, in nature and in history, preserving, sustaining, and governing the created order."[4] Calvin writes that "God is not just momentary creator who has finished his work. That would be cold and barren. He sustains, nourishes and cares for everything he has made, even to the least sparrow. God's omnipotence is not an empty, idle and almost unconscious sort, but a watchful, effective, active sort, engaged in ceaseless activity. He regulates all things - nothing takes place

---

[4] John H. Leith, *Basic Christian Doctrine* (Louisville: Westminster John Knox Press, 1993) 81.

without his deliberation. He exercises special care over the order of nature and over each of his works. Nothing takes place by chance."

There are so many stories I could share with you about the providence of God, like when I was getting ready to take a group of girls from my church in San Angelo, TX to the Great Escape in Gunnison, CO. I was to be the only adult with 5 teenage girls. I was to drive the church van the 13 hours the next day. Herman, our church custodian, asked if he could check out the van for me, fill it up, clean it, check the oil, etc. I told Herman that was not necessary, that someone had taken it last week to prepare it for the trip. Herman didn't listen to me. He went and checked out the van anyway, and come to find out, our brake line had been cut and our spare tire stolen. Herman was usually very cooperative. Why did he go ahead and do what I told him he didn't need to do? Providence. I believe the Spirit of God compelled Herman to check out the van to keep us safe and off on time the next day.

Or what about when my family moved from Texas to Georgia? I was afraid we wouldn't fit in. I was afraid we wouldn't find people like us there. I found out after we got there that, of all things, a female pastor taking a break for mothering attended my church. She did so with her non-clergy husband, her 4th grade daughter (the same age as my daughter at the time) and her preschool son adopted from Thailand. We were instant friends.

How did she end up at my church or I at hers? Was it chance? No. It was providence. The God who cares what I think and feel, the God who knew what I needed supplied a good friend by arranging this occurrence. You know what I am talking about: that person you ran into; that check that came in the mail just in time; that coincidence whose odds against it happening were astronomical, all helping and guiding you to God's provision and blessings in your life. It's providence.

Providence stands against doctrines that define our lives in terms of chance or fate, astrology or natural law. George Barna tells the story of the overstressed elder in a small church that lost its pastor. He fretted over what they would do and whom they would find, only to have a new minister accept the congregation after only a brief search. Somewhat embarrassed by his lack of faith and prayer during the interim, he "only half-jokingly" wisecracked: "As luck would have it, providence was with us!" Providence rejects any dependence upon good luck.

It may be helpful at this point to talk about what providence is not. Providence does not mean the divine predetermination of historical events. It just means events in our lives will be affected by God's wisdom, grace, and power. Remember when Joseph's brothers sold him into slavery? Joseph's words to them, when he met them much later as second in command in Egypt, affirm God's providence. He tells them, "Even though you intended to do harm to me, God intended it for good" (Genesis 50:20). Providence does not deny that bad things happen. What it affirms is that "all things work together for good for those who love God and are called according to his purpose" (Romans 8:28).

God's providence also does not relieve us from responsibility. What do birds do all day? They look for food. Jesus and everyone listening to his teaching knew this. God feeds them and yet all day they look for food, as they must do. God has set limits on our lives and entrusted us with their care. God has provided means and helps to preserve our lives; God has also made us able to foresee dangers. God has given us the responsibility, as creatures made in his own image, of living life responsibly and of acting justly and mercifully toward each other.

Providence is not the jingle, "Don't worry - be happy." Providence invites us into the kingdom of God "where in both good and bad times, we have no reason to worry. Jesus tells us that the life of faith is not without its issues, concerns, and challenges. There are setbacks, delays, detours, failures, frustrations as well as joys, triumphs, victories and accomplishments. The point is that when we are about God's business, we have no room or need for worry. Everything is in God's hands and we are assured we can handle whatever happens, because God is in control.

Few of us are exempt from worry and anxiety. Most of us worry about losing homes, jobs, not having enough for retirement, caring for our children, avoiding danger, and terrorist attacks, just to name a few. Jesus understands this. His call to worry-free living is not based on unrealistic views of the world. His words are for those who understand that God will not leave us without His presence and help. We can face life with all its contingencies and uncertainties with the assurance that we are not alone, that God hears, sees, and cares about each one of us. Don't worry - because God is in control."[5]

When I've been the most thankful that I knew about the providence of God is not when I was in the easy times of my life, when everything was as it should be and I could say, "See, God has provided for me and blessed me." It has been in the hardest times that the providence of God gave me the hope that allowed me to make it through. I learned this lesson from my father when I was twelve years old. He had a disappointment in his career. An expected promotion did not happen. And so, what did he do? He didn't mope

---

[5] Barbara J. Essex "Matthew 6:24-24" *Feasting on the Word* Year A Vol 1 (Westminster John Knox Press, 2010) 408.

around, or yell, or complain about the injustice done to him. He sat his family down and told us that whatever happened, we were all in God's hands. He shared a poem with us that I have never forgotten.

It goes like this:

Disappointment – His Appointment

Change one letter and you'll see

What I view as life's disasters

Are God's perfect plan for me.

I believe, because of the teaching of Jesus, the record of Scripture, and experiences in my life, that God loves me and desires the best for me - not necessarily what I want, but what God wants to make me into the person He has called me to be. God is always loving, caring, guiding, protecting, and preparing me and all who love Him for the wonderful things "no eye has seen, nor ear heard, nor heart even conceived."

Can I believe this? When someone cuts me down or doesn't appreciate my gifts? When I get bad news or a disappointing outcome? When I fail? When a disaster happens? When someone that I love is slowly dying and my prayers seem to go unheard? Yes, I can. Faith, Calvin tells us, is a firm and certain knowledge of God's benevolence toward us. It is founded not on happy thoughts or a positive attitude. It is founded upon the freely given promise in Jesus Christ our Lord. The one who is teaching us about birds and grass is the one who was crucified to redeem it all. And when my faith waivers, I consider again what Jesus suggests, the lilies of the field and the little birds at my feeder, and I again trust the loving Father who so gently feeds and cares for all creation. Believe that in every event in our world there is always God's grace, wisdom, and power at work. Don't worry! Believe in the providence of God for you.

God Is Not Fair!

Matthew 20:1-16

I am a justice-loving person. I get upset when things are not fair, but much in this world is not fair, and this is probably not a news flash to anyone here. That is why I love movies where justice prevails. One of my favorites is *Double Jeopardy*. In it a man fakes his own death, and his wife is convicted of his murder. She finds out he is alive and a fellow inmate tells her that she can only be convicted of his murder once, so when she gets out she can kill him in cold blood. I find myself rooting for her. I want her low-life husband to get what he deserves.

I think people like these movies because they have experienced injustices in their own lives. I remember in my first semester of seminary I took a class called Ministry in a Cultural Context. We met once a week and a majority of the grade was participation. Two of the three hours we met were small group discussion of our readings. Attendance was mandatory. Of course, I attended every class. I read every word assigned. I worked and researched above and beyond the requirements on my papers. My friend John who was also in the class was a senior. He rarely read the books assigned and he showed up for four of the twelve class meetings for the semester. I ended up with an A- in the class. I was pleased with my grade until I found out that John got an A- as well. There is no way we could get the same grade I stewed to myself. I worked so much harder than he did. And ever since then, thinking about that class leaves a bad taste in my mouth. Maybe you have a similar experience, an experience where you were not rewarded for hard work and someone was rewarded who did not deserve it.

This is the complaint of the first group of laborers in our story. The landowner is not fair. He has not paid them justly. They worked hard all day and received a day's pay. But those who worked less, even those who worked much less, received the same. It is not fair. I must say that their complaint is valid. Or at least is appears to be after one reading.

The story of the vineyard workers is a parable. Jesus used parables to teach about the kingdom of God by drawing a metaphor between common life and the kingdom of God. Parables can be hard to decipher and leave sufficient doubt in the minds of the disciples and in ours as well about their precise application.

So, what does this parable tell us about the kingdom? Surely it is not an exhortation to arbitrarily pay workers, nor to fight against injustice. I believe this parable tells us that God's kingdom works on the principles of grace. And the principles of grace offend us initially, for the benefits of grace are not rewarded based on the merit of the recipient, but on the merit and generosity of the giver. No matter our performance or the age at which we begin to work for God's kingdom, we are all equally valued and welcomed by God. As we look more closely, we realize that the landowner was not unjust. The landowner lived up to his oral contract with the first laborers. He paid them exactly what they were promised. The first group had no argument with what they were paid. They argued against others getting the same. The first group was not mad because of an injustice, they were mad because of kindness, because of the landowner's generosity with the other workers. And come to think of it, I was not upset about my A-; I was upset about John's A-. We humans think that we want justice for all instead of the kindness of the landowner. We argue that the system of grace doesn't work. It encourages laziness. It encourages others to have fun, wait until the end of day to work, and still receive the same. This system of grace does not reward those who faithfully work all day.

Or maybe it does. You see the first laborers were so worried that someone else got the same pay at the end, that they missed what they had gotten in addition to the denarius. They got to be in the vineyard all day, instead of at the day labor pick-up spot. They got to work side by side with the landowner. They even got to know him. They now know the feel of a grape and exactly how to hold their hands to pick. They learned to pick faster and faster. They got to marvel at the beautiful colors and forms of the grapes and their vines. They got the satisfaction of seeing the harvest from start to finish. They became friends with those who worked all day with them. They shared stories and laughed and took breaks together. And all day, they had the security of knowing they were employed and that they would be paid. If you have ever been unemployed, you know what that means to someone.

Did I just receive an A- minus in that class I took? No, for I gained knowledge and insight. I was able to discuss and debate with colleagues from Latin America, from Africa, and from Hungary, colleagues who were black and white, single and married, Methodist, Presbyterian, Pentecostal, and Unitarian. I was able to hear the gospel in their own words, from their point of view. I was able to read the book of Job with those who have suffered injustice. I am a better pastor and person because of my work in that class. And because of my pouting about another's' grade, I almost missed the joy of this realization.

Friends, what joys would you have missed if you had not been working for the Lord all day? Would you have missed the joy of seeing your children baptized or confirmed? Would you have missed seeing the excitement in a child's face as they learned for the first time that the lions didn't eat Daniel? Would you have missed the chance to pray for healing and see it happen? Would you have missed the chance to drastically change someone's life by giving to a helping ministry? Would you have missed the thank you from the person you served at the soup kitchen? Would you miss knowing your whole life that you were loved passionately by your Maker? Would your life be different if you spent your life not knowing that you were of infinite worth because you were made and redeemed by God? Mine would. And we will miss these things if we are busy comparing our work in God's kingdom to others.

It is so easy in the life of the church to notice what others are not doing. Friends, there is always a lot of work to do in God's kingdom. Join in and do not worry about what others are doing or not doing. Do not miss the joy of working by complaining about others.

The truth is we all need generosity and kindness. Sometimes those in the church forget that we too depend upon the generosity of God because we too will find ourselves unworthy of the pay at the end of the day. Who here hasn't attempted their best only to find out that there was better? And who here hasn't wondered what happens when what we promise to God and what we produce aren't even close to being the same? Do we realize that every breath that we take is a gift from a loving and gracious God? And do we understand that, no matter what, God will give us what we need at end of the day? That's what this parable proclaims to us. God is not fair! God is generous. Thanks be to God.

What Is Your Name?

Luke 8:26-39; Galatians 3:23-29

What do you say when people ask you your name? It depends on the situation. My name is Tracey, Pastor Tracey, Mrs. Jack, Davenport, mom, Rev. Dr. Tracey Davenport (in formal, professional settings), honey, Trace, sugar plum to Jimmy, Stacy to some who mix me up with their grandchildren, and finally sometimes "C" to my husband, which I will not explain (it's an obscure biblical reference). Names speak volumes about who we are, how we see ourselves, and how we interact with the world. We call people names that indicate our relationship and view of them, both good and bad. I've been called some beautiful names and some awful ones. Names matter.

We find Jesus in our gospel reading for today asking someone their name. Jesus and his disciples have crossed the Sea of Galilee, surviving a windstorm to reach this man in pagan territory. He's a man possessed by demons, running around naked in a cemetery, unable to be held. I wonder what the people of his town called him? Crazy? Idiot? Loser? Retard? Sinner? Someone who got what they deserved?

Jesus asks him, "What is your name?" Many people assume Jesus was asking the demon. I don't think so. I think Jesus was asking the man his name to assess his well-being. That man was so far gone he couldn't even answer. The demons jump in to answer Jesus: "Legion!" This poor man had so many competing interests in him he didn't know who he was anymore.

That's what the demonic does to us. Demons "thrive in chaos, confusion, and competition." They are the structures and functions that dehumanize us and cause us to be victims. These powers will try anything to separate us from the love of God. Demons want to estrange us from God and our own higher self, the image of God in us, and get us to ignore who we truly are. Walter Wink, a theologian who wrote a lot about these demonic powers, attests to the fact that he knows the voice of demons saying to him, "You're no good and you will never be any good." He has heard the hateful liar telling him he is worthless, not precious to God, not beautiful, not loved.[6] Humans feel this life-quenching power, desiring to suck us down into feelings of worthlessness, despair, and to kill us both physically and spiritually. Once we forget or ignore who we truly are, then we are lost and find ourselves not living, but running around among tombstones, called every name in the book but our real name.

That's why Jesus came. Scripture tells us that: "The reason the Son of God appeared was to destroy the works of the devil" (1 John 3:8). Jesus directly confronted the demonic in people's lives with exorcism and healing. Jesus very presence expelled the lies within this man and called forth his real self. We find him then sitting at the feet of Jesus, clothed and in his right mind.

Long before this man was a crazy person, long before he lived like a rabid animal in cemetery, he was beloved child of God. Truer than any condition he may have, more right than any other label society had given him, he was a beloved child of God. Even with a hundred villagers afraid to approach him, even with a thousand competing voices telling him he was a lost cause, he was a beloved child of God.

---

[6] Walter Wink, *Unmasking the Powers: The Invisible Forces That Determine Human Existence* (Philadelphia: Fortress Press, 1986), 27.

Whether he never knew it or had long forgotten it, it was still true and that knowledge changed everything.

Once we know and believe this about ourselves we must know and believe it about other people – people who are different from us, people who may scare us, people who live across the sea in unknown territory. Jim Wallis wrote a piece this week called *A Theology of Love and Hate, from Charleston to Orlando*. He recounts: "We have seen the appalling and frightening depths of hate that human beings can descend into. Far beyond disagreement, debate, and opposition to one another's ideas or behaviors, hate degenerates into vicious attack, verbal abuse, and physical violence against other human beings. Ultimately, the violence of hate is the denial of the image of God in the other human beings we have decided to use, abuse, and even kill. "Whoever does not love does not know God, for God is love." (1 John 4:8). Hate is not only the anti-thesis of love; hate is the anti-thesis of God."

Just a week ago, Omar Mateen entered a gay nightclub in Orlando and shot and killed 49 people and wounded at least 53 others. Omar seems to have been a mentally unstable and violent man who shouted his allegiance to ISIS as he murdered one person after another. Omar allowed other voices, demonic voices, to name him. Omar did not know who he was. Long before he was a follower of a violent extremism, long before he was mentally ill, he was a beloved child of God.

Omar also ignored who the people in the club were. I don't care if you support or oppose gay marriage. That is beside the point. It is vital that we Christians, who know our real name, "stand up for the safety, humanity, and dignity of LGBTQ people,"[7] and all people, as

---

[7] https://sojo.net/articles/theology-love-and-hate-charleston-and-orlando

beloved children of God. If Jesus is our example, and I believe he is, then we must love them. Long before we are gay or straight, we are beloved children of God. That's why, according to the Associated Press, Chick-fil-A employees in Orlando served food on Sunday after this gay nightclub was attacked, breaking with the restaurant's tradition of remaining closed on that day for religious reasons. They made food for people waiting in line to donate blood after the massacre. This time they opened on Sunday for religious reasons. They know everyone's real name.

This awful tragedy has also caused many to spew hateful rhetoric about Muslims. This breaks my heart because I have multiple Muslim friends. They are good, kind, amazing people. They have helped me in many ways. Those who live in the United States love it here and are so thankful for the freedoms they have and the opportunity for success. Long before we are Muslim or Christian or Jewish, we are beloved children of God and until we learn to see each other and treat each other as such, we give evil its opening to try to make us less than we were created to be.

One year ago, Dylann Roof, filled with the hate that he'd been taught, entered an historic African Methodist Episcopal Church in downtown Charleston, S.C. Jim Wallis recounts the story: "Invited to join in by members of the church, the young man sat at the table during the Bible study then pulled out a semi-automatic handgun and killed nine Christians as they started to pray, including the senior pastor, Rev. Clementa C. Pinckney. . . Those killed were shot multiple times at close range while Roof shouted racial epithets at his victims. He had the wrong name for those precious people!

"But at the legal hearing for the killer two days later, both survivors and relatives of five victims spoke to Dylann Roof directly. They told the young white supremacist who killed their families and friends that they forgave him and were 'praying for his soul.' The nation was stunned again with the totally unexpected power of love and forgiveness."[8]

Christians responded to the tragedy at Mother Emanuel in Charleston with acts and gifts of love. We sent cards – do you remember? We did so because we know those Christians, our African American brothers and sisters, are beloved children of God. Long before we are ever black or white, before we are Asian, or African or North American, before we are Presbyterian or Baptist, Roman Catholic or Pentecostal, we are one in Christ Jesus.

Fear cannot overcome evil. Hate cannot overcome evil. Only good can overcome evil. Only bold acts of love can overcome violent acts of hate. One bold act we can all engage in is to remind people of their real name. You are a beloved child of God. The more we hear it, the more it will sink in. The more it sinks in, the more we are found at the feet of Jesus in our right minds. The more we are found there, the more we will go and tell what God has done for us. The more we go and tell, the more the world will know our and their true name.

Christians in the United States can no longer ignore the evil and oppression affecting so many in our world. When we do acknowledge it, though, it is easy to fall into despair and a sense of helplessness at the way the world is today. We sometimes mistakenly believe there is nothing we can do about problems as big as war, terrorism, gang violence, or slavery or as personal as family problems, drug addictions, and racial prejudice. At this point we must remember that the battle is already won. "The resurrection symbolized not only that Christ overcame the evil of his day two

---

[8]https://sojo.net/articles/theology-love-and-hate-charleston-and-orlando

millennia ago, but that he overcame it for all time."[9] This is how the New Testament speaks of it, as if victory has already occurred: "He has rescued us from the power of darkness and transferred us into the kingdom of his beloved Son, in whom we have redemption, the forgiveness of sins" (Col 1:13); all authority on heaven and earth has been given to him (Mt 28:18); Jesus is Lord (Acts 2:36).

Shirley Guthrie writes, "The confession that Jesus is Lord does not mean that we can sit back with a sigh of relief and tell ourselves that everything is all right now. The powers of evil around us and within us have not yet admitted defeat. The risen Lord is still finishing the work he began, and to call him Lord means to throw ourselves into the battle with him."[10] When we know of violence to anyone – physical, emotional, or spiritual, let us do what we can to protect and stand with those who are victims and heal them. When we hear someone called a loser, addict, has-been, nuisance, weirdo, fatty, fag, stupid, sissy, pig, drunk, idiot, and the like, let us go to them and tell them that first, before any other name, they are called "my beloved child" by God. Let us treat all people as such. See what it does for them. See what it does for you. See what it does for this violent world. Can you imagine what might happen if all two billion people on this planet who claim the name Christian did this?

"What is your name?" Jesus asks each one of us in an effort to heal us and make us whole. What do you say?

---

[9] M. Scott Peck, *People of the Lie: The Hope for Healing Human Evil* (New York: Touchstone, 1983), 205.
[10] Shirley C. Guthrie, *Christian Doctrine: Revised Edition* (Louisville: Westminster John Knox Press, 1994), 286.

God's Things

Luke 20:20-26

The question we read about today is a tricky one: "Is it lawful to pay taxes to the emperor or not?" The Pharisees and Herodians butter Jesus up with praise for his wisdom and then lower the boom. They were trying to trick Jesus, for either way he answered the question someone would be unhappy. If Jesus answered yes, it is lawful to pay taxes, then the Jews would accuse him of idolatry. The denarius at that time had upon it the image of Tiberius Caesar, the reigning emperor. The title inscribed upon the coin read "Tiberius Caesar, the divine Augustus, son of Augustus." On the reverse would be the title "pontifex maximus", the high priest of the Roman nation. To pay taxes or homage to Caesar was to engage in emperor worship. But, if Jesus said, "No, do not pay taxes to Caesar" the IRS would get him.

Jesus, as wise as he is, does not answer their question directly. Instead he gives a principle to live by. Having given this principle, Jesus leaves it up to the hearer, both then and today, to struggle to relate this principle to their own life and work out its implications. In other words, Jesus wants us to use our brains. "Give to the emperor the things that are the emperor's, and to God the things that are God's" is Jesus' answer to their question.

So, we must find out just what are God's things? What belongs to God? If we listen to the Psalmist, the whole earth is the Lord's and all that is in it. Everything belongs to God because God made it. There is nothing that doesn't belong to God. If everything belongs to God, then we are merely stewards of what we have. A steward is someone entrusted with the management of the affairs of a household or estate of an owner. A steward is not at liberty to use what he or she is given as he or she so pleases. A steward has no right to dispose of anything that is in his or her hands but only according to the will of his or her lord. Whatever we do with what is in the world, we are charged to do according to God's will and purpose. Everything we have in material possessions, property, money and in the environment belongs to God and we are merely stewards of it. We give a small portion, a tenth, back to God, but the real question for stewards is not what we are going to give back, but what are we going to keep and what are we going to do with it? God has made us partners in the administration of the things we have been given.

What if we believed that? What if we believed that all we had belonged to God? Would we take better care of it? Would we share more of it? Would we open our home or volunteer our car for the youth group to use? Would we house visiting missionaries or speakers? Would we offer rides to those who could no longer drive? Would we take better care of the earth? Would we waste less water and energy and recycle our trash? Would we invest more in eternal things that seem to be higher on God's priority list than in temporal things? Would we pray and seek God's wisdom in Scripture before we spent any of it? Or would we just be so very much more thankful for what we have? It's up to each one of us to answer these questions.

I am pushed by this passage to something else that belongs to God. Notice the reasoning Jesus' uses when contemplating the question about taxes. He asks for a denarius. He asks the Pharisees and Herodians, "Whose image (Greek: *eikon*) is on this coin and whose title?" I think Jesus is deliberately alluding to Genesis chapter 1 verse 27 which reads: So God created humankind in his image, in the image of God he created them; male and female he created them.

We bear the image of God, and therefore we belong to God. Our whole lives and all that they encompass belong to God, because we bear God's image, no matter how distorted that image may be.

We belong to God. In life and in death we belong to God. We belong to God not as slaves but as children, bearing the image of our Father and with the ability to bring honor or dishonor to our family name. What if we believed that? If we believed that we bear God's image and thus belong to God, how would it affect our behavior? Would we abuse our health with a bad diet and lack of exercise? Would we start to get enough sleep and take a Sabbath one day a week? Would we have a better self-image, knowing that our lives have value and meaning and a purpose because we are stamped with God's image?

What if we believed that we belonged to God, bearing his image? Would that change how we did our homework or housework, or our jobs? Would it affect who we voted for or if we voted at all in national and local elections? What does a steward of democracy do with it? Would a belief that each of us belongs to God change our spiritual life and growth and commitment to it? We can't ride the coattails of our parents or our children or our mate forever. There comes a point where each of us must have our own daily walk with our Creator; our own personal relationship with Jesus Christ; and our own sense of the Holy Spirit in our lives. No one else can do it for us.

God has created us as bearers of his image to be in personal relationship with him in response to his love. We must have our own personal prayer life, our own personal encounter with the Bible, our own theology and personal faith. Somewhere along the way we must stop and figure out what we believe in, what we are committed to, and what the real priorities are for us. We can't just go through the motions or put in our time, or "play church". Each of us must make his or her own decision to give our life, our whole life and all it entails, to God. Life as one made in God's image, as described by the Confession of '67, "is a gift to be received with gratitude and a task to be pursued with courage." We are free to seek the purpose of God in our lives. We are stewards of that purpose.

In this sermon of endless questions, I have just a few more. What if we believed that other people belonged to God because they bear God's image too? If we believed that blacks and whites and Latinos and Asians all bear the image of God, how would we treat each other? What about Israelis and Arabs? Don't they all bear God's image? If we believed that others belonged to God and that our things were God's things, what would we do if we heard about a need? Would we help with food and shelter or a Christmas present? Would we take the time to get to know each other better? Would we defend and fight for each other when oppression became heavy?

Friends, the thing that will enable us to be good stewards of our material goods and our lives is the knowledge that all that we have and all that we are belongs to God. People with cancer, and AIDS, and addictions to narcotics are God's. The misbehaving child in your Sunday school class belongs to God. The irritating co-worker and the rebellious son belong to God, bearing God's own image. We all must wrestle with and live out what that means. Jesus doesn't give us an easy answer. He gives us the principle: Give to God the things that are God's. Let us use this week to wrestle with the questions and be good stewards, both as individuals and as a church, of God's things.

Justifying Ourselves

Luke 10:25-37

I wrote a Christmas letter last year. Here is how it went:

Dear family and many wonderful friends,

I am writing to you from our luxurious home in serene Severna Park, Maryland, where we enjoy the calm, quiet beauty of the trees and birds, yet are never too far from the educational and entertainment advantages of a big city like Baltimore. As I look outside my window now on this beautifully autumn, but not too cold day, I see happy young children riding bikes on the sidewalk, careful not to hit the flowers around my mailbox. They wave at me as they pass by my window.

Enclosed is a picture of the whole family wearing matching sweaters I knitted myself. Jack is still employed in a crucial and high paying position, yet is able to spend plenty of quality time with family and friends. Taylor and Alia attend one of the finest schools in the nation, both making straight A's. However, Alia's verbal exuberance is a challenge to the teachers who are obviously not trained to handle a child with such gifts.

Our church is wonderful. The pews are full, even in the summer and on holiday weekends. Everyone attends Sunday school and we have a waiting list to become a teacher. All families tithe, giving the Biblical ten percent of their income to the church. Everyone is overjoyed to try new hymns and songs that I pick to enhance our worship experience. It could not be more wonderful.

I must go now to begin baking homemade goodies for all I know. We will then begin packing for our Christmas holiday in the Caribbean. I hope you are as happy as we are.

Justifying ourselves,

Tracey, for the whole Davenport family.

Have you even gotten a Christmas letter like this? I have. Humans somehow need to have others know how wonderful they are and how great they are doing. A Christmas letter is a perfect vehicle to pretend that we are wonderful and that everything is great.

The lawyer in our story today was just the same. A discussion with an up and coming rabbi is just the vehicle to highlight how well he is doing. He wants to inherit eternal life. He answers Jesus' question correctly. He knows the formula: "Love the Lord your God with all your heart, and with all your soul, and with all your strength, and with all your mind; and your neighbor as yourself."

But wanting to justify himself, our text says, he asks another question. Wanting to justify himself. Wanting to show himself to be acceptable to God and others. Don't we all want to do this? To show ourselves to be acceptable to God and others? He wanted Jesus to clearly define the limits of his duty so that he could check off the requirements and be sure he had fulfilled them.

Jesus doesn't give a straight answer. Jesus tells a story, a parable. This has become the most famous story Jesus ever told. It begins with a certain man, could be anyone, who is traveling the road from Jerusalem to Jericho. It is a road that is steep and winding, descending 3300 feet in 17 miles. The narrow passes and terrain offered easy hiding for bandits. Robbers attacked him, stripped him, beat him, and left him for dead.

A priest sees the robbed and beaten man and passes by on the other side. One would expect a clergyperson to stop and help. Jesus doesn't tell us why he didn't stop. What went through his mind? Maybe it was something like this: *I have spent weeks at the Temple serving God and I'm on my way home to see my family. My family needs me. According to the law, I am not allowed to touch a dead person. He may be dead. I will get dirty. It could be a trap. I have no way to transport him. I cannot carry him all the way to Jericho. It is best if I just pass by.* In his mind, he justified himself for not stopping.

A Levite happens along and probably uses the same self-justification for not stopping to help. Perhaps the Levite sees the priest pass by, and is influenced by his example. Finally, a Samaritan comes along. A Samaritan was considered by this lawyer and all listening to Jesus to be unclean, socially outcast, and a religious heretic. He was the opposite of the priest and Levite, a person who had no way whatsoever to justify himself. The Samaritan is the one who stops to help and who is the example of a good neighbor.

A famous theologian lecturing at Harvard Divinity School stood up and asked the students, "With whom do you identify in the parable of the Good Samaritan?" Some admitted that they were like the priest and the Levite. A few argued that their faith had made them like the Good Samaritan. The theologian, after the students were done telling and explaining all their answers said this: "You are all wrong. You are the man in the ditch."

Arthur McGill expounds on this revelation. He writes that we are not the Samaritan in this story. We are the anonymous bloodied nobody lying helpless in a ditch. We are the needy. There is no way we could ever justify ourselves. Any snotty Christmas letter is only pretend and an outrageous exercise. The Good Samaritan is none other than Jesus Christ himself who finds us, heals our wounds, and provides for our needs. Conversion is just the discovery of this Great Friend and our ability to see ourselves as those in a ditch. This is what makes us good neighbors. It is our wisdom that understands "there but for the grace of God go I" which compels us to help. When we are looking down on others, there is no way to see God. When we look up, we see others and God. If we are busy stockpiling and safeguarding our sense of self with possessions and illusions of control, we will never see ourselves or others as we should.

Maybe the hated Samaritan knew what it was like to be cheated and beaten by the world. Maybe he knew what it was like to be in a ditch. Nothing like a little ditch time to give us compassion for others and make us good neighbors. Nothing like giving up trying to justify ourselves will open our eyes to the plight of others.

Maybe you have been in a ditch lately. Everybody has at one time or another. Cancer is a pretty big ditch. Unemployment and financial difficulties are ditches. Failure at marriage, parenting, or anything else is a ditch. Alzheimer's is a ditch for all involved. Rejection is a ditch. Sin is a ditch, both our own and others sins against us. Sometimes the world hits us and robs us over and over and over again. It is Jesus who sees us and refuses to pass by. Jesus comes over, lifts us up, tends our wounds, and refuses to ask whether we are worthy of his help. Jesus is moved with compassion for all who hurt. He is moved with compassion by your hurt and longs to help you out of the ditch. That is the meaning of this parable: to get the lawyer away from justifying himself and to see the gracious act of mercy and grace that God has done in Jesus Christ for all who need help. We all need help.

There is one character left in this story. It is the one we should strive to be. The innkeeper is the one to whom the Samaritan brings the rescued man. The innkeeper, at the request of and with payment from the Samaritan, graciously cares for the wounded man until he is well. I wonder if the innkeeper wasn't the last man the Samaritan found in the ditch? I wonder if he hadn't been rescued himself and knew the goodness of the Samaritan? You see, he keeps the wounded man on the promise of payment when the Samaritan returns. The innkeeper keeps the man, at possible expense to himself, trusting in the faithfulness of the Samaritan. He must have known something good about the Samaritan.

We know that Jesus is faithful. We know that we have been rescued from the deepest ditch of all by him – the ditch of sin and death. We know that there is no use justifying ourselves before God or others. It is God who justifies us in Jesus Christ. So, that is why we are more than willing to help those who Jesus brings to us. That is why, even if it costs us something – time, energy, or money – we will help. Jesus will not give us a list that we can check off. He gives us a command: "Love the lord your God with all your heart, soul, strength and mind and love your neighbor as yourself. Do this and you will live." "Who is our neighbor?" we ask. It is anyone Jesus brings to us for care.

My real Christmas letter will read like this:

Dear friends and family,

We write to you to wish you a very Merry Christmas and a Happy New Year. We are so thankful to have good jobs and good schools. We are thankful to be part of church that loves us, despite all our faults, and loves the Lord. We are thankful most of all this Christmas for our Great Friend Jesus.

You are always welcome in our home. If you need any help, let us know. We'll be there.

With love and gratitude to God,

The Davenports

The Most Generous Man in Town

Luke 19:1-10

There are things that frustrate me greatly about being a pastor of a church and the number one thing is that so many Christians don't understand what "being the church" is supposed to be. Some think the church should be the moral police of our society. We set the standard for behavior and condemn all those who do not follow our standard. You know I believe personal righteousness to be extremely important for the lives of Christians and the well-being of society, but if the church were supposed to be the morality police, then we would have seen Jesus going around telling all these sinners where they went wrong. Instead, he ate with tax collectors and sinners. The only people Jesus condemned in the gospels were the self-righteous religious leaders.

Others see the church as an institution that provides religious services: sacraments, classes, sermons, worship services, musical offerings, weddings and funerals. Some are willing to pay for these services, and some partake without every offering anything in return. When this is one's mindset, the church becomes cold and faithless. The church becomes nothing more than a business. The church leaves the One we claim to follow behind. We fail to make disciples of Jesus.

The church is called to be a community of believers growing out of the grace of God in Jesus Christ our Lord, who because of that grace, together follow Jesus Christ, acting as his presence in our world. This paradigm for church is so beautifully illustrated in our reading for today.

Zacchaeus was the chief tax collector of Jericho. Tax collectors in Jesus' day were collaborators with the enemy occupiers and almost always overcharged, making themselves rich in the process. Ironically, the name Zacchaeus in Hebrew means "just". The people hated him, calling him a sinner. They were not his friends and were not going to let that little twerp in the front of the crowd to see this most famous Rabbi come through town.

For some reason, Zacchaeus had to see Jesus. I think it was because Zacchaeus had looked at his own life and was not happy. I believe Zacchaeus was looking for help because his dissatisfaction with his own life had become stronger than his power or wealth. He is now insecure, even in his powerful position and financial security. He cannot go to his friends for help – he does not have any that are not tax collectors. He cannot go to any normal rabbi; they know him as a sinner, as a person far from God with no hope for help. But Jesus is a different story. Jesus, he heard, even has a former tax collector named Matthew as one of his own disciples. Maybe Jesus is the one who can help him.

So, Zacchaeus takes the chance. He throws aside all personal and professional dignity and climbs a tree to get a look at Jesus. He will be made fun of – his shortness accentuated by his tree climbing. But he does it anyway. It is worth the risk. What happens next is the very essence of the gospel: Jesus, who was supposed to be passing through town, stops, looks at Zacchaeus in that tree and invites himself over for dinner. The way Jesus treats this no-good cheater is incredible. Instead of pointing a finger of scorn, Jesus' hand was extended in friendship. Instead of pouring out insults, which by now I am sure the crowd was doing, Jesus was inviting himself to Zacchaeus' home. Instead of saying, "Stay up in that tree by yourself where you belong," Jesus said, "Come down and take me home with you." Zacchaeus is captured by the grace of God in Jesus Christ.

This outpouring of grace changed Zacchaeus on the inside. The crowd was not pleased with what Jesus did, offering himself to Zacchaeus in an uncritical, accepting way. The crowd grumbled. But Zacchaeus welcomed Jesus with joy. Then, in the most amazing turn of events, Zacchaeus' responds to Jesus' loving outreach to him. Zacchaeus changes. The theological word for this is repentance. I think that when Zacchaeus knew that Jesus was for him rather than against him, knowing what kind of life he was living, he was able to admit where he was wrong and decide that he wanted to change. Zacchaeus was not being forced to decide one way or the other, but as he sat there in Jesus' presence, he knew that he would be lost if he simply went on in the same old way.

Grace then changed Zacchaeus on the outside. The crookedest man in town, by just being in the presence of Jesus, became the most generous man in town. Jesus didn't have to chew Zacchaeus out with moral platitudes. Jesus didn't offer a religious formula or service. Jesus just loved him as he was. It was then that Zacchaeus chose to change, to start a new way of life. Zacchaeus went well beyond Torah requirements which require restitution to those defrauded plus one-fifth. Zacchaeus, the former white collar criminal, become the model of generosity, giving away half of all he had to the poor and restoring four times what he took in fraud.

I have found what Jesus insists upon and the gospel proclaims to be true: Grace changes people – more than anything else could. Max Lucado writes about it saying, "Grace comes after you. It rewires you. From insecure to God secure. From regret-riddled to better-because-of it. From afraid to die to ready to fly. Grace is the voice that causes us to change and then gives us the power to pull it off."[11]

In one of my favorite angel movies *Michael*, the archangel Michael uses a parable to explain to a reporter how he works. He says, "The north wind came to the sun and said, 'I bet I can make that man down there take off his coat faster than you can. The sun agrees. The north wind blew and blew and the more it blew, the tighter than man held his coat around him. Then, the sun smiled upon the man, warming him and the man released his coat.'"

Zacchaeus was warmed by the grace of Jesus, and so could release all he previously held onto. Zacchaeus' inward transformation led to his outward transformation. That no-good tax collector became the most generous man in town.

"We distort the doctrine of salvation," David H.C. Reed argues, "when we make it primarily an other-worldly doctrine. A truncated view of salvation diminishes God's power and presence in the present moment. Salvation is the change of heart and action. Encountering Jesus' love and receiving it into our hearts results in a changed life, this very day. It's God's love and kindness that lead us to repentance (Romans 2:4). Repentance is about recognizing what is wrong, and making it right. Zacchaeus repented, because of the love and power of Jesus Christ." Zacchaeus became the grace of God in his generosity to others.

I saw something here last Sunday that makes me think Harundale is different than the other mainline churches, that we might be getting what grace is all about. The Presbyterian Women were having their fall luncheon and business meeting. I was last leaving the church that

---

[11] Max Lucado, *Grace: More Than We Deserve, Greater Than We Imagine* (Nashville: Thomas Nelson, 2012), 8.

Sunday except for them. As I was leaving I encountered a woman I did not recognize sitting in our hallway. I asked her if I could help. She said no. She said she was waiting for the library to open at one o'clock and could she please sit there until it did because it was so cold and windy outside. I smiled and said, "Today you're in luck. Normally I would have to lock the building, but since our women are still here, you can stay until they have to lock up." She thanked me.

I let our women know that that this woman was out in the hall waiting, that I told her she could stay there until they were finished. I went to my car and realized I had forgotten something. I came back in to notice the Lounge doors open and this woman, who had been in the hall, going through the buffet line and then sitting at the table with our women. They had come out and invited her in.

Now they had every right to say, "This is our meeting. This is our food." They would not have been judged in any way for just letting that stranger sit in the hallway, warm until the Library opened. But I believe that because those women have been captured by the grace of God in Jesus Christ and changed on the inside, they had to be generous on the outside. They had to be what the church should be. And they were. I drove home so very proud and thankful.

When's the last time you were overwhelmed by God's grace? When's the last time your insides were changed? When is the last time your generosity overwhelmed someone else? Maybe it will happen today. Jesus has once again invited himself to dinner with us, with all of us who are unworthy, who have not led exemplary holy lives, who are not perfect. Will you join him? Will you allow his presence to change you on the inside? Will you then use your life to follow him and become some of the most generous people in town? May it be so!

The Ghost of Christmas Past

Luke 3:1-16

Today we are visited by the Ghost of Christmas Past. When I think of Christmases past, I remember an accidental tradition with which I grew up. Wherever we lived, we always had a fireplace, and since we lived in mostly warmer climates it remained unused expect for Christmas Day. No matter how warm it might be outside on that day, my father always awoke at 5am to light a fire in the fireplace. I guess he was hoping to add that cozy, fireside atmosphere to our present-opening and breakfast eating. Unfortunately, the atmosphere he created was one of yelling, grouchiness, and ungratefulness for his efforts. Every year, he forgot to open the flue. What resulted was a smoke-filled living room and smoke detectors going off, arousing all in the house. As the years went by, it got to be a joke, because he always forgot.

I couldn't wait to celebrate my first Christmas after Jack and I were married. We had a little apartment in Dallas, TX. We had a small Christmas tree, with colored lights. We had a fireplace. Jack arose early to light a fire, the first one in that fireplace, as we had just moved in a month earlier. I remained asleep in bed until I awoke to the familiar Christmas sound of a smoke alarm. Jack had forgotten to open the flue. This I surmised was a cycle from which I could never break free.

John the Baptist appears confronting God's people with the cycle from which they had not been able to break free. "You brood of vipers!" he calls them. We don't see many Christmas cards with "You brood of vipers" on the front. "Even now the ax is lying at the root of the trees; every tree that does not bear fruit will be cut down and thrown into the fire." This is not the most popular of Christmas messages. Repent. Change your mind. Turn around and go the other direction. That is John's message. It confronts those who will hear with all the mistakes, all the regrets, all the disappointments, all the sins of the past.

Israel had been unfaithful to God time and time again throughout their history. They had worshiped other gods. They had failed to keep the commandments. Leaders had become corrupt, taking bribes, losing any sense of justice and righteousness. They did not defend the widow, the orphan, or the stranger in their midst. Then the unthinkable happened. God allowed the northern tribes of Israel to be captured by the Assyrians. God allowed the southern tribes of Judah to be overtaken by the Babylonians. Jerusalem was destroyed, temple and all, and God's people were taken into exile in Babylon. There in a foreign land they wept and longed for Zion.

Charles Dickens describes Ebenezer Scrooge as a "squeezing, wrenching, grasping, scraping, clutching, covetous old sinner." Dickens goes on: "Nobody ever stopped him in the street to say, with gladsome looks, 'My dear Scrooge, how are you? When will you come to see me?' No beggars implored him to bestow a trifle, no children asked him what it was o'clock, no man or woman once in his life at all inquired the way to such and such a place of Scrooge. Even the blind men's dogs appeared to know him, and when they saw him coming would tug their owners into doorways and up courts." "No warmth could warm, no wintry weather chill him. No wind that blew was bitterer than he."

Scrooge became this way over years and through experiences past. Scrooge learns through his dead former partner Marley, that his past is a heavy chain around him, of his own making. The Ghost of Christmas Past is sent to Ebenezer Scrooge, for his own welfare it claims, to confront him with his past: all the mistakes, all the regrets, all the disappointments, all the sins.

As the Ghost of Christmas Past escorts him, Scrooge sees himself as a solitary child in school, neglected by his friends. He sobs at the sight. He sees himself, a boy whose only friends are characters in books, and he cries, "Poor boy," wishing he had given something to the poor boy singing Christmas carols at his door last night. He sees his sister, who loved and cared for him as a boy, yet was never appreciated by him. He had turned her son, his own nephew, away that very day. He sees his agitation at the merriment of his boss one Christmas in his young adulthood. He regrets that he has not made this season more joyful for his own clerk, Bob Cratchit. He sees Belle, a beautiful young woman, who loved him, and who he rejected for the lure of wealth.

Scrooge can take no more from the Ghost of Christmas Past. "Remove me from this place," Scrooge asks in a broken voice. The Ghost replies, "I told you these are shadows of things that have been. They are what they are. Do not blame me." "Remove me," Scrooge shouts back. "I cannot bear it."

Our past is our problem too. We like Scrooge may break no law and be quite safe from prison. But we, like Scrooge, can be miserable human beings, all wrapped up in ourselves and enjoying making others miserable. We all have chapters in our lives we had rather forget. We all have not lived up to our potential. There are decisions we regret and missed opportunities that in hindsight, we grieve we missed. There are Christmases past when we shut out someone who should have been included and we cheated them out of our love and company. There are Christmases past where we may have been the one shut out. There are those in need from whom we have withheld the blessings God has given us to share. There are times I have behaved badly, and knew it, but did it anyway. I have not been worthy of my calling as a minister of the gospel. There are years past when God was shut out of our lives. When we are confronted with all these things, and aware of the damage done, we too like Scrooge cry out, "I cannot bear it! Show me no more!" We too like the crowds listening to John the Baptist ask, "What shall we do?" Is all lost? Do we give up and spiral down into depression and despair? Do we quit trying?

Amidst tears falling and hearts breaking come the words of the Lord through the prophet Isaiah, "Comfort, O comfort my people. Speak tenderly to Jerusalem. Prepare the way of the Lord. Every valley shall be lifted up and every mountain made low." "I will redeem the past," says the Lord. "I will make it right. I will make a way for you to come back home smooth and straight."

We sing songs during advent as a people who have realized our past is a chain around us and need the salvation God offers. *O come, O come Emmanuel and ransom captive Israel. From our fears and sins release us; let us find our rest in Thee. God rest ye merry gentlemen let nothing you dismay. Remember Christ our Savior was born on Christmas Day to save us all from Satan's power when we had gone astray. O tidings of comfort and joy.* We need Christmas because of our past. Christmas doesn't come because we worked ourselves up to it, or because we deserve such a favor. God came to us in Jesus Christ because we needed it, because we are a sinful lot, a brood of vipers. Jesus came because we needed help. The message of Christmas is that our past can be redeemed. We can change. We can be transformed. We don't have to stay in chains of addiction, bitterness, sin, shame, or despair. We don't have to keep repeating our mistakes.

Do you remember how the story of Ebenezer Scrooge ends? He is converted. He becomes a new man. The man who violated Christmas the worst becomes the man who keeps it the best.

My favorite Christmas story has always been *How the Grinch Stole Christmas*. It is because the worst offender, after experiencing the love and joy the Who's in Whoville experience at Christmas, becomes the chief celebrant. "And he, he himself, the Grinch carved the roast beast."

These supposedly secular stories proclaim the good news of the gospel that began with Christmas. If Scrooge and the Grinch can be changed, then so can we. We are never too old, too young, too cold, or too far gone to confront our past and be free of it. God makes the way to be free, to come home, to redeem anything that is wrong, broken, and disappointing.

Maybe it's a strained family relationship that needs to change. Maybe its bad choices or harsh words said in haste. Maybe it is a sense of entitlement or a lack of compassion. Maybe it's a heart, like in the case of the Grinch, is two sizes two small. Whatever it is that needs to change, to repent, or to be made right, take comfort. We will see God's salvation: a tiny baby born and laid in a manger. This baby's words will teach. His hands will heal. His life will be an example. This baby's sweet little head will one day wear a crown of thorns. This baby's blood will be shed for us. This baby will redeem the past and make us holy. This is the good news of the Ghost of Christmas Past. The past does not have to be the future. Praise God!

The Ghost of Christmas Present

Luke 2:1-7

Christmas Day, 2002, my family set off from Georgia on a car trip back to Texas. We were looking forward to being back in Texas, even if just for a little while. We woke up early Christmas morning, opened presents, ate breakfast, and loaded our car. After a late lunch, Jack and I, Taylor and Alia, and our two little dogs headed west on I-20, hoping to get to Jackson, Mississippi to spend the night. We got to Tuscaloosa, Alabama around 7pm. Needing something to eat we drove around off several exits to find that everything was closed. Fast food, gas stations, convenience stores, even the Chinese Buffet Palace were all dark. We were getting desperate. We wasted almost an hour looking for somewhere or something to eat. We were all hungry and tired and it seemed we would find nothing. Finally, just as we had given up, we saw a light shining in the darkness. A neon sign was lit off the last Tuscaloosa exit, beckoning us to come closer. It was an eating establishment and they were open. We had a good meal. The workers and other customers were festive and friendly to us. But this was not the Christmas night meal I had envisioned. We ate our Christmas night meal, celebrating Jesus' birthday, at Hooters.

If you knew me well, you would know how Hooters would be the last place I would ever want to eat. Being vehemently against women parading around in scanty clothing, it is the last place I would want my husband and children to go. Hooters is a scandalous place for any clergyperson, male or female, to be found. God has a sense of humor; no doubt about that. It wasn't perfect. It was a Christmas night I could have never imagined. And yet we were together; we had been provided for; we celebrated that God was with us in Jesus

Christ; we were full of joy. Years later, we are still laughing about that night.

Luke tells us briefly of the trip that Joseph and Mary took on what is now known as the first Christmas. After a long trip to Bethlehem because of the census, they arrive in Bethlehem to look for a place to stay. "Hotels in their day would make even the most meager of our contemporary economy motel chains look luxurious."[12] Hotels back then were a serious of thatched rooms or porches, built around a common courtyard. They were dirty, uncomfortable, badly kept and badly managed. Innkeepers had a bad reputation, because inns were so often used for immoral and criminal acts. This is the sort of place to which Mary and Joseph came to ask for a room.

Have you ever shown up without a reservation to see the desk clerk shake his head negatively? Have you even been where you thought you could drive no further, but unable to find a place to spend the night? It is unpleasant enough in a car, but imagine if you or your spouse were nine months pregnant and you were traveling on a donkey? A stable at this motel was all that the last possible stop had, and so a stable they took.

It still seems like such a simple and beautiful scene; the way Luke tells it. "While they were there, the time came for her to deliver her child. And she gave birth to her firstborn son and wrapped him in bands of cloth and laid him in a manger." We lay out the beautiful picture in our nativity scenes. But, we must know Luke leaves out a lot of details: Joseph's frantic preparations to help a woman give

---

[12] J. Ellsworth Kalas, *Christmas from the Back Side: A Different Look at the Story of Jesus' Birth* (Nashville: Abingdon Press, 2003).

birth (something he was not supposed to do), Mary's screams, the blood and cutting the umbilical cord.

The first Christmas wasn't perfect. Jesus was delivered by a man who didn't have a clue what he was doing. Jesus, the Son of God, came into this world the same way all of us do. He came to a place that didn't have room for him, the smelly stable of a seedy motel. And yet God was there. Joseph and Mary were together; they had been provided for; and Jesus their promised child was here, safe and sound. God was in their present, even though it wasn't perfect, to bring help and peace and joy.

The Ghost of Christmas Present comes to Ebenezer Scrooge and escorts him to the Christmas celebration of his clerk Bob Cratchit. The family's clothes are worn, but have been dressed up with new bows. They cannot afford a big goose, but act as if they are having a feast to end all feasts. Bob has several children, one of whom is disabled and, as Scrooge finds out, terminally ill. Yet Scrooge sees that everyone has enough to eat and that they are full of joy in the holiday of the birth of their Savior. He sees the whole family gather around the hearth after dinner. Bob raises his cup, as high as any golden goblet, and exclaims, "Merry Christmas to us all, my dears! God bless us!" which all the family echoed back. "God bless us, every one!" said Tiny Tim, the last of all. They sang together a round of joyous songs. Dickens writes, "They were not a handsome family, they were not well dressed, their shoes were far from being waterproof, their clothes were scanty. But they were happy, grateful, and pleased with one another."

Scrooge is then led to a place where miners work and live. The Ghost of Christmas Present exclaims, "See, they know me." Scrooge finds them a cheerful assembly, around a glowing fire, singing Christmas songs of joy. Scrooge finds the same on a ship far from shore and at his nephew's house. "Much they saw and far they went, and many homes were visited, but always with a happy end. The Spirit stood beside sickbeds, and they were cheerful; on foreign lands, and there were close at home; by struggling men and they were patient in their greater hope; by poverty and it was rich. In almshouse, hospital, jail, in misery's every refuge, where vain man in his little brief authority had not made fast the door and barred the Spirit out, he left his blessing." The Ghost of Christmas Present showed Scrooge that where Christmas is celebrated, where Christ is born anew, no matter the situation, there is joy. Scrooge had wealth and everything he thought he wished, and yet was without the joy that Christmas brings.

Where are you this Christmas? Are you home or away from your true home? Are you overworked or looking for work? Are you healthy or ill? Are you rich or poor? Are you overwhelmed with company or lonely? Do you find yourself at Hooters or in a stable or somewhere you never imagined? Our move to Maryland has not been perfect. It is always difficult to move to different place. But Jesus is Emmanuel: God with us. God is present with us here. God has provided abundantly for us: a place to live, a marvelous and kind church family, and his love and grace poured out and overflowing through us.

If you saw the email from Najla, our church's former intern who is now serving in the National Evangelical Synod of Syria and Lebanon, you heard the same. "Despite all," she writes, "we are assured of Immanuel: God with us, even when we fail to see clear signs . . . For unto us a child is born!"

The good news of the Ghost of Christmas Present is that no matter where we are, Christ can be born there. Just because things are not perfect, do not assume God is not there. Life will not be perfect. No

Christmas was ever perfect. But Christ can be born and celebrated in any situation and bring more joy and peace than we could ever imagine.

Can we welcome the Ghost of Christmas Present and the joy it will bring? Or have we made fast the door and barred the Spirit out? Can we learn that welcoming the Ghost of Christmas Present will do to us what it did to Ebenezer Scrooge when he awoke? "I don't know what to do!" cried Scrooge, laughing and crying in the same breath. "I am as light as a feather. I am as happy as an angel. I am as merry as a schoolboy. I am as giddy as a drunken man. A Merry Christmas to everybody! A Happy New Year to all the world! It's Christmas Day! I haven't missed it." May we never miss it!

The Ghost of Christmas Yet to Come

Luke 21:25-36

This passage from Luke is about what is commonly referred to as the Second Coming of Christ. It is also known in Scripture as "the great and terrible day of the Lord" and in theological circles as the Parousia. Christians believe and confess that Jesus will come again to the earth. How much time we spend thinking about it, discussing it, or focusing on it depends largely on denomination. It also depends upon where we are in history. As Luke was writing this gospel, the destruction of the temple in Jerusalem had just occurred. This was a cataclysmic event that signaled the beginning of the end for those who lived at that time. For us, the advent of the year 2000 spurred many articles, books, and discussions about the Second Coming.

Scriptures tells us precious little about the Second Coming and the end times of history. It most certainly does not tell us when it will happen. Cosmic signs will appear, but they have always appeared. In 1982, the planets around the sun were in perfect alignment. This was sure to be the dawning of a new age, at least for all of us who grew up in the 60's and 70's singing songs from the musical Hair. The truth is that no one knows when it will be. Even Jesus said he not know the day or the hour, only his Father in heaven knew when it would be.

With so little detail about the Second Coming, with no knowledge about when it will be, and with it taking so very long after the first coming, what's the big deal? Should we be worrying about it or talking about it at all? Yes, I believe we should live expectantly for the day of Christ's second coming, just as we lived expectantly for the celebration of Christmas, the anniversary of his first coming. Thinking in terms of a returning Lord is vital to the Christian life.

The reality of the Second Coming means that God isn't finished with history yet. We live in a time theologians call "the already and the not yet." Already, the kingdom of God has broken into this world. Jesus Christ has come and lived among us, showing us how we should live as God's people. He has accomplished a mighty victory over sin, death, and evil upon the cross. He is risen and seated at the right hand of God the Father. He is already King of Kings and Lord of Lords. But, we do not yet enjoy the fullness of the kingdom and of life only as it will be known when King Jesus returns. Things will not be as they are. There will come a day when wars will cease, when the lion will lay down with the lamb, when there will be no more death. There will come a day when we will see Jesus, whom we have worshiped and adored, face to face. Thinking about that day gives us hope. It keeps earthly gains and losses in perspective for us. It means that history is not some meaningless evolution or repetition of the past; history is headed toward a goal: the universal reign of Christ, when every tongue will confess Jesus Christ as Lord. Waiting for such a day gives God and us time to work toward that goal.

During the worst of times in the Revolutionary War in our country, Abigail Adams, who was living outside of Boston, wrote to her husband every day. He was in Philadelphia arguing out independence with the Continental Congress and believing that Great Britain would surely crush them before they ever got started. He was gravely discouraged until he received these words from his wife: "The race is not to the swift nor the battle to the strong, but the God of Israel is he that giveth strength unto his people. Trust in Him at all times." God was not finished with these 13 colonies yet.

If we look, we can see God moving and working in our world today. We can find glimpses of the miraculous, of faithful obedience, of love conquering evil in a multitude of situations. God is not finished with Pakistan or with Iraq. God is not finished with Israel or Palestine. God is not finished with the United States yet. History isn't finished until Jesus comes back.

On a more personal and less cosmic level, the Second Coming means that God isn't finished with us yet. Whether we are 9 or 99, God is not finished with our lives. God is, right now, working all things together for good for those who love him and are called according to his purpose. There is preparation in us to be done. As long as we live, we continue to ready our hearts, minds, and spirits to stand before the Son of Man on that day. Jesus exhorts us to be ready for the day when he will come again.

The Ghost of Christmas Yet to Come comes silently to meet Ebenezer Scrooge. Without saying a word, the spirit shows him the future, and the lonely death of a man despised by all. He sees the dead man's belongings, stolen and pawned by his servants. He sees the dead man lying in his house with no kind word spoken of him. He sees men who will attend his funeral, only for the free food. He sees his own gravestone. Worse than that, he sees Bob Cratchit's family mourning the death of Tiny Tim, thanking God for his short but happy life. "Answer me one question," said Scrooge to the spirit. "Are these the shadows of the things that will be or are they shadows of things that may be only?" Still the ghost pointed to the grave by which they stood. "Men's courses will foreshadow certain ends, to which, if persevered in, they must lead," said Scrooge. "But if the courses be departed from, the ends will change. Say it is thus with what you show me!" The spirit said nothing. "Spirit," Scrooge shouted, "hear me. I am not the man I was. I will not be the man I must have been to lead to this. Why show me this if I am past all hope?"

Scrooge heeded the warning of the Ghost of Christmas Yet to Come. He changed in his ways. "Scrooge was better than his word," Dickens writes. "To Tiny Tim, who did not die, he became a second father. He became as good a friend, as good a master, and as good a man as the good old city ever knew. It was always said of him that he knew how to keep Christmas well, if any man alive possessed the knowledge."

Have you made any New Year's Resolutions yet? I encourage you to make them this year mindful of Christmases yet to come. What kind of person do you want to be? What do you want to do with your life? What can you do to change the history of the world? One member shared with me that her New Year's resolution is not diet and exercise (as it has been in years past) but to love her enemies. O my friends, that kind of resolution will cause changes inside of her, outside of her, and maybe even change the history of the world. There is no telling what God will accomplish in you and through you before Jesus comes again.

When Jesus came the first time, there were cosmic signs: a strange star over Bethlehem at his birth, an earthquake and darkness at his death. When the second coming is imminent, there will be cosmic signs and great distress. It will be so bad, Jesus said, that people will faint from fear. Not us. We are the ones who are looking forward to that day, expecting that day, getting ready for that day. We will stand up and raise our heads high, because our redemption is drawing near. We will be ready to meet the one whose birth, death, and resurrection we have celebrated for thousands of years. We will meet the Son of Man not as one to be feared, but as a well-known and welcome friend who will finish the work he started when he came the first time: the final destruction of death and evil. In the meantime, in the in-between time, remember that God isn't finished yet, not with the world, and not with us.

The Poll Numbers Are Up

Matthew 21:1-11

It is the Sunday before the Passover, and Jerusalem is full. Jesus, the prophet from Nazareth, has been making his way toward Jerusalem for some time now. Jerusalem is the city about which great promises are made to the people of Israel. Jerusalem is the place where the Messiah will enter, according to the prophet Zechariah, triumphant and victorious, yet humbly riding on a donkey. This is it! This is the day that Jesus will take his rightful place.

A very large crowd gathers spreading their cloaks on his donkey, spreading cloaks and palm branches along his path into Jerusalem, a sign of honor. The people are yelling, "Hosanna, Save us!" The people are invoking King David's name in reference to Jesus. I can imagine just what the disciples are thinking and saying to each other: Can you believe this? This is it. We have picked the right rabbi to follow. Look at this crowd! The poll numbers are up. Jesus is sure to win the election, if there was one. Everybody loves him! We have never seen a crowd like this! Jesus will march into Jerusalem and the Romans will have to flee. Jesus can ride this tide of popularity all the way to the top. Even Rome cannot stop him now.

The disciples were all caught up in the celebration and were wrong about Jesus' popularity. It was fleeting. When he entered Jerusalem, the story says, the whole city was in turmoil. Many in the city were frightened, disturbed, and made anxious by Jesus' arrival. Any quest for power and authority by Jesus would be met with a strong response by the Roman authorities. Jesus' teachings and ways threatened the religious leaders' traditions and privileges. He is a hillbilly from Nazareth. What does he know about leadership? What does he know about politics? Who does he think he is?

In many ways, we are like both groups. At times, we hail Jesus as king and celebrate his arrival. We live in a place where it is easy to openly worship, throwing our cloaks and branches on the ground in respect. It costs us nothing to show up with the rest of the crowd and give lip service to our allegiance to Jesus. It makes us feel good to be in such a crowd. We, like they, have high expectations. We know the miracles Jesus has performed. We know who he claims to be. We desperately want what only he can give us. "Hosanna!" we shout. "Save us!"

But at the very same time, we are disturbed by his presence. We are nervous and fearful. Jesus is riding into the center of our lives. What will that mean? What is Jesus going to upset? What resistance will he stir up?

What if Jesus becomes king in our families? How would we have to treat each other? If Jesus took over, it would mean we would treat each other with love and compassion. Husbands and wives, parents and children, brothers and sisters giving instead of taking, forgiving instead of holding grudges, nurturing, holding each other accountable, respecting, modeling sacrifice and generosity. All our relationships would be under his rule. We are not sure we want them to be. Who is he anyway? What does he know about family life in 21st century America?

What if Jesus rode his donkey right into the middle of our work? Do we want Jesus messing with what we do for a living and how we earn our money? Do we want him asking questions about quantity and quality, about justice and mercy, about fair compensation and loyalty, about righteousness and honesty? He's a hillbilly from Nazareth. What does he know about what it takes to get ahead in corporate America?

What if Jesus rode his donkey right into the middle of my heart? What would he see? Would he, as rightful king, denounce the pride, the jealously, the delusions of grandeur, the bitterness, the stinginess, the sense of entitlement, or my own self-righteousness? Do I want Jesus stirring things up? What if I am happy the way I am?

What if Jesus rode his donkey right into the middle of our church? What would he want to change? We don't like change. What programs would he criticize? What would he challenge us to do? What would he like? How much more inviting and accepting would he want us to become? How much more truth would he have us speak? How much more would he ask us to give? He might come in here and wreak all kinds of havoc. Do we want that? If his poll numbers were up when he rode in, the minute he started changing things, they would go down. What kind of leader is he anyway?

Jesus tells his disciples just days before his entry into Jerusalem, "You know that the rulers of the Gentiles lord it over them, and their great ones are tyrants over then. It will not be so among you; but whoever wishes to be great among you must be your servant, and whoever wishes to be first among you must be your slave; just as the Son of Man came not to be served but to serve and to give his life as a ransom for many." (Matthew 20:25-28) In other words, "greatness comes in what you do for others and who you are for those who need you."[13] Jesus will not be swayed by his rising poll numbers. He will not be enticed by power or popularity. Jesus is the kind of leader who will be obedient to his Father. He will sacrifice for those he serves.

For us then, to follow him as king we must be obedient. The call to discipleship is the call to live as Jesus directs, to do God's will instead

---

13 Grant, R. Charles.

of our own. Our goal becomes to please God instead of pleasing ourselves. The road of obedience is a hard road to travel. There is no promise that it will be easy; that all will go smoothly; or that the wind will always be at our backs. Only those who have tried it know how hard it is to love one's neighbor. Only those who have tried it know the difficulty in doing justice and loving mercy at the same time. Only those living a very sheltered life believe that resisting the temptation to fulfill all our own desires, to go with the crowd, or to amass power and wealth for ourselves is not a fight to the death.

Theologian James R. Edwards writes, "The more we obey God, the more real God becomes to us and the greater our love grows. And the more we love God, the more we become like God. There is something about love that is no longer love apart from obedience. Obedience is not a penalty levied on faith. It is the strength of faith." Dietrich Bonhoeffer insists repeatedly in *The Cost of Discipleship* that, "Only those who obey can believe, and only those who believe can obey."

This Sunday, Jesus' poll numbers are up. Crowds are ready to crown him king. But in his obedience to God, they will go down. Way down. And on Friday, only a few will even say they ever knew him.

For us to follow Jesus as king, we must be willing to sacrifice for others. We must be willing to give our time, our money, our energy, our minds, our hearts, our hands and feet in the cause of this king. Part of me wants to do a sales number that says, "Come on and follow him. Everybody join the party. It's easy. It's fun. It's free. It requires nothing on your part. Jesus will give you everything you want and more." That would keep Jesus' poll numbers up. But it would be a lie. Jesus said, "If anyone wants to become my followers, let them take up their cross and follow me. For those who want to save their life will lose it, and those who lose their life for my sake, and for the sake of the gospel, will find it." (Mark 8:34-35)

We will probably never be called upon to lose our physical lives in service to Jesus. But we are called to live lives of sacrificial service and humble obedience each day. One thing we must remember, however. Obedience and sacrifice are never the end. They, as part of God's great plan, always lead to glory. Obedience and sacrifice always lead to something far better than we ever could give up, something far more wonderful than we could even imagine. Because Jesus was willing to be obedient to the will of his Father, because he willingly laid down his life, he is now exalted above every other name, and one day every knee in heaven and on earth and under the earth will bow to him and every tongue confess that Jesus Christ is Lord, to the glory of God the Father. Because he was willing to sacrifice himself, we are saved.

Today, the poll numbers regarding Jesus are up. The crowds are crying, "Hosanna to the Son of David! Blessed is the one who comes in the name of the Lord!" He is beautiful. He is powerful. He is popular. It will not last. Things will get worse before they get better. The poll numbers will go way down. The road will seem impossible at times. The crowd will turn on him. Even his best friends will betray and deny him. He will be mocked, ridiculed, beaten, and crucified. He will die a cruel death, in physical, emotional, and spiritual agony. What are we going to do? Are we going to follow him or turn away?

Dead or Alive?

John 11:1-44

There is not one person here who cannot grab onto this story and wish it were true. There is not one person here who has not been affected by death – the death of a parent or grandparent, the death of a child, the death of a dear friend. Either as welcome relief from suffering or an untimely accident, death is a universal. There is nothing humans can do to avoid it or conquer it. We are all going to die. We have tried with our technology to prolong life, and even to create life. We have also blurred the line between life and death. Is life a heart beating? On its own or with assistance? Is life brainwave activity? Are we sure we can tell what constitutes life and death? Even if we can, there is no technology to beat death. We continue to try however, because there is something inside of us that fights it. We are programmed to want to live.

In this story from John, Jesus reveals three things about death. First, **death is not the end of our existence**. Jesus describes Lazarus' death as "falling asleep". The disciples misunderstand what Jesus is saying. Then he must tell them in their own language. Lazarus is dead. But, this is not the first time the disciples have heard death described as falling asleep. Mark and Luke record the miracle of Jairus' 12-year old daughter being raised from the dead. Remember when Jesus arrives at the house, the mourners are weeping and wailing. Jesus says, "Do not weep; for she is not dead but sleeping." The mourners laugh at Jesus, until he takes her by the hand and calls out, "Child, get up!" Her spirit returned and she got up at once. There was an early Christian hymn that Paul quotes in his letter to the Ephesians that sings, "Sleeper, awake! Rise from the dead." We even get our word cemetery from a Greek word, which means "sleeping place." In Jesus and the early church's understanding, death was not annihilation, but just a change, much like falling asleep and then being awakened.

Secondly, we learn from this story that **Jesus hates death**. Note how Jesus reacts to death and its effects on those left behind. When Jesus sees Martha weeping, verse 33 describes Jesus as greatly disturbed in spirit and deeply moved. Jesus is not happy with this situation. He is angry and agitated at the affects death had on this family whom he loved deeply. Jesus also weeps on the way to Lazarus' grave. He is not just shedding a tear. Jesus is weeping, sobbing, at the death of his friend. If there is one thing we can take from Jesus' reactions here it is that Jesus is against death. The fact that we humans die is not the way Jesus wants it. This is not the way it was supposed to be.

The third insight the story of the raising of Lazarus teaches us about death, sickness, or any difficult situation is that **the best course of action is to appeal to the love of God in Jesus Christ**. Notice the wording of the note that Mary and Martha sent to Jesus: "Lord, he whom you love is ill." The note did not say, "Remember Lazarus, how good Lazarus was and what great faith Lazarus had?" It did not lay out why deserved to be healed for the good of the community. It simply said, "He whom you love is ill." The point is that Jesus loved Lazarus. This is much like telling a parent that their child is hurt. All you have to say is, "Your child is hurt." The parent does not need to hear all the details or evaluate the child's obedience or loyalty before they run to help. The plea for help appeals to the parent's love for that child, not that child's worthiness to receive it.

The story of the raising of Lazarus not only tells us something about death, but also something about life. First, **Life is person**. Life is not the condition of a beating heart and breathing lungs. All throughout this gospel, Jesus has claimed to be necessary for life. He promised the woman at the well living water. He said, "I am the bread of life." Jesus said, "I am the resurrection and the life." Life is a person and real life can be had only by joining the one who is Life. Life with and in and through Jesus Christ is abundant, eternal life.

Second, **the life that is ours in Jesus Christ does not end with our physical death**. Jesus said, "Those who believe in me, though they die, will live." Yes, we still die physically, just as Lazarus eventually died again, physically. But, physical death for the one joined to Christ is just a passage, a promotion to finally see what has been true all along: though we die, we will live. When Dwight L. Moody was close to dying, he said, "Someday soon you will read in the papers that D.L. Moody is dead. Don't you believe it! At that moment, I shall be more alive that I am now." To die is gain.

Third, this story shows us that **eternal life starts now**. Jesus said that everyone who lives and believes in Him will never die. Jesus is saying that just as life does not end with our physical death, it does not start there either. From the moment, we take Christ and the Life that He is, we are alive. We are alive in Christ now. We use terms for believers like born again, regenerated, and new creation to describe this. The promise of the resurrection is not some distant event at the end of time as Martha supposed. It is a reality for us the moment we are united with Christ. This life with Christ that we live now is real, abundant and eternal.

The promise of life is an invitation. "Do you believe this Martha?" Jesus asks? Do we believe this? It is rather hard to believe that Lazarus was raised after being dead for four days. It is an outrageous story to many in the 21st century. I can tell you that there were about a hundred witnesses to this miracle. Or I could argue that the Pharisees did not dispute this miracle. In fact, they believed it so surely that from that day forward they plotted to kill both Jesus and Lazarus for being sorcerers. But, a better question than do you believe that Lazarus was raised is: Do you believe that God, acting in Jesus Christ, has power over the course of live and death? Do you believe that Jesus is the resurrection and the life? If Jesus is, then this Lazarus incident was a piece of cake. Our God can make dry bones live. Our God makes dead things alive. And if Jesus is who he claimed to be, the resurrection and the life, then anything in your life that is dead and in the grave can be made alive in Jesus Christ, no matter how rotten it has become. Do you believe this?

I believe that Jesus is who he claimed to be. I believe it for the same reason that we worship on Sunday and not Saturday. I believe because Jesus himself went into death and came out alive, not to die again as Lazarus did, but to live forever. Do you believe this? Do you believe that God in Jesus Christ has the power of Life over death? I do. So someday when you read or hear that Tracey Davenport is dead, don't you believe it!

On a Mission from God

Matthew 28:16-20

In the 1980's, when I was in college, there was a movie called *The Blues Brothers*. It's a great story about the redemption of paroled convict named Jake and his brother Elwood, who take an amazing journey to save the Catholic orphanage in which they grew up from being closed. To do so they must reunite their blues band and organize a concert to pay the orphanage's debts. Along the way, they are hampered by all kinds of obstacles and enemies, and relentlessly pursued by the police. But no matter who tried to stop them, Jake and Elwood kept going, they faced their enemies head on, and their mantra became: "We're on a mission from God."[14]

James Meredith, who led two major events during the American Civil Rights Era (desegregating the University of Mississippi in 1962 and leading the March Against Fear in 1966, which helped open the floodgates of voter registration in the South), had this to say about his role: "I am not a civil rights hero. I am a warrior, and I am on a mission from God."

Our denomination is shrinking. The whole of the Christian church, both mainline and evangelical in the United States is shrinking. It is growing by leaps and bound in Africa and Asia, but here it is not. Many have suggested theories on why this is so. I believe it is because we have been so busy fighting each other, that we have not answered the call of our mission from God. We have not done the evangelism (yes, I said that word) our faith compels.

---

[14] www.astillsmallvoiceofcalm.blogspot.com , Jun 11, 2013.

The call in Scripture is clear. From the call to the prophets like Jeremiah to Paul's beseeching of the early church, we are to be witnesses to who God is and what God has done. How will anyone know if we do not tell them? The last words of Jesus before he ascended into heaven were instructions for his disciples. These words are called "The Great Commission" and it is an amazing mission from God for the disciples of Jesus: make more disciples. Baptize and teach them. Go out in my name to the world and bring them into this family. This should be easier for us than telling someone about your favorite book or movie or liking something on Facebook. "Telling another person about God's love in Jesus Christ and the difference that has made in our lives should be the easiest thing of all. But most of us have not found this to be easy. We worry about what to say. We wonder how our words will be received. We are uncomfortable talking about ourselves. We are concerned about intruding into another's space. And we certainly don't want to sound judgmental." [15]

We have also witnessed such awful examples of Christians who are disrespectful with those who disagree, hateful toward those who do not follow their way, and harmful to our faith by not showing the love of God in Jesus Christ our Lord. Do we want to be lumped into the same category as the Westboro Baptist Church? Certainly not!

We have not always found it so difficult. I heard the Moderator of the Presbyterian Church (USA), Dr. Heath Rada, preach last week. He reported on our missionaries and shared that 94 million Christians in the world today attribute their faith in Jesus Christ to the testimony and work of the PC (USA). That's amazing! So how

---

[15] Boyd Lien, *Engage: Gospel Leader's Guide* (Louisville: Witherspoon Press, 2013) 3.

do we, the "frozen chosen" do it? How do we carry out our mission from God?

Live the life of faith. Saint Frances implored us to preach the gospel at all times, and if necessary use words. We can't share faith if we don't live it. Non-believers can spot a hypocrite a mile away. Hebrews tells us that "faith is the assurance of things hoped for; the conviction of things not seen. Without faith, the writer continues, it is impossible to please God, for whoever would approach him must believe that he exists and that he rewards those who seek him" (Hebrews 11:1, 6).

Teacher Brennan Manning shared the following: "In the forty-eight years since I was first ambushed by Jesus in a little chapel in the Allegheny mountains in western Pennsylvania, and after literally thousands of hours of prayer and meditation, silence and solitude over those years, I am now utterly convinced that on Judgment Day the Lord Jesus is going to ask us one question, and only one question: *Did you believe that I loved you, that I desired you, that I waited for you day after day, that I longed to hear the sound of your voice?*"

That's faith! To borrow Paul's words to the Roman church: Faith is believing that God is for us. To quote Calvin: Faith is a firm and certain knowledge of God's benevolence for us. And what does a life of faith look like? If we believed God loves us, longs for a relationship with us, and waits for us, who might we be and what might we do? Would the world's accolades and rejections carry the same weight? Who would we aim to please? Would we care about the welfare of others or look out for just ourselves? Would we treat those different from us with love and honor or with hatred and contempt? Would we loudly condemn the sins of others or would we take the log out of our own eye first? Would we love our enemies and pray for those who persecute us? Would we use our bodies and brains, our gifts and talents, our resources and time on things that matter or things that don't? (If you knew the time, energy, and expense to which I have gone to root on the Baltimore Orioles . . .) Would we spend time talking to God or not? Would worship be a priority or not? Not that we will be perfect. But what is our norm? Is it a life that speaks the peace and confidence that comes from being sure of and secure in God's love? Is it a life that follows Jesus as our example? Believing changes the way we live and work and interact with our world.

O my friends, our lives will speak who we are and what we believe. The world will watch and know if we believe the good news of the gospel. We are all witnesses. We may be good witnesses or bad witnesses, but we are all witnesses. We don't have to say a word.

Secondly, when it is time to say something, **don't be afraid to speak up, but always speak with humility and respect**. In the first letter of Peter, he writes, "Always be ready to make your defense to anyone who demands from you an accounting for the hope that is in you; yet do it with gentleness and reverence (1 Peter 3:15-16). *The Message* translation puts it this way: "Be ready to speak up and tell anyone who asks why you're living the way you are, and always with the utmost courtesy." When we live lives of faith, people will ask. We need to be ready to tell why we live the way we do.

Why aren't you more upset about the news from your doctor? *Because Jesus is the Prince of Peace and he is my best friend. I am in God's very capable hands. Can I tell you about him?* The stock market is crashing. Why aren't you depressed? *Because the King of the Universe is my Father and I don't have to worry. The Lord is my Shepherd; I shall not want! Can I tell you about the amazing ways he has provided for me in the past?* Why are you friends with that loser? *Because he's not a loser. He is a beloved child of God! Would you like to be part of family that welcomes everyone?* Why do you operate your business ethically? If you just fudged the numbers a little bit . . ." *Because I answer to a God who calls for justice to flow down like mighty waters and righteousness like and ever-flowing stream and who gives me the strength to do the right thing.* Why do you spend so much money and time helping those in need? *Because we follow Jesus and he said that whatever we do for the least in our community we do for him. Would you like to know more about what Jesus did and said? Would you like to volunteer?* You lost your job. Why aren't you suicidal? *Because I know a love so real and so strong that one job doesn't determine my worth. God so loved the world that he gave his only begotten Son for us, for me. Do you need a love like that in your life?* Why do you wake up so early on Sunday morning and go to church? Why not sleep in or relax and play some golf? *Because I know a love so real and so strong that I can't help but go and worship and praise and thank and listen to and give to the God I know. Would you like to go with me sometime?*

If we live the life of faith, we will be asked. Be ready with your answer. It is our mission from God. Our testimony will make disciples.

And finally, on our mission from God, it is crucial to **know that we are not alone.** It was true for the first disciples, going out in the name of the Father, and of the Son and of the Holy Spirit. It is true for all of us, as Jesus promised in our reading for today: he is with us always. The grace of our Lord Jesus Christ, the love of God, and the fellowship of the Spirit do not stay here. When we go out, they go out into the cold, hard world in which we live. Don't be afraid.

One of the saints of Harundale Presbyterian Church and one of our choir's great sopranos, a leader on Session and one of the best Bible teachers was Joan Sell. Joan got lung cancer, even though she never smoked a day in her life. As she became sicker and sicker, I struggled with how to help her. As strong a believer as she was, there is nothing scarier than not being able to breathe. About that time, a song came out on Christian radio by Chris Tomlin. His song proclaims in the chorus: *I know who goes before me. I know who stands behind. The God of angel armies is always by my side. The God who reigns forever, he is a friend of mine. The God of angel armies is always by my side.*[16] I shared these lyrics with Joan who was more of a Baptist hymn kind of person than a contemporary Christian music kind of person. But she heard them and thought about them. The next day when I went to see her, she reported to me and her daughters that at one point during the night when she was scared and couldn't get her breath, even though she was alone, she felt a hand rest on her arm. A strong hand. A peace-giving hand. She knew the Lord was present. She was not alone. Her fear fled.

Joan told us about this experience. She told all her nurses and doctors. Joan told her church friends and her hospital roommates and their families. Joan was on a mission from God to proclaim the peace she received from God in the midst of her awful situation.

We are all on a mission from God. We have a calling to make disciples. And so, we live the life of faith, we are ready to speak with humbleness and respect, and we know that we are not alone. If our church can do this, we will grow in faith, in strength, and in number (although that is the least important of the three). If Christians will do these things, the gospel will spread like wildfire like it did when the first disciples received this mission from God.

---

[16] Chris Tomlin, *Whom Shall I Fear?*

The Talking Donkey
(and Other Animals in the Kingdom)
Numbers 22:21-35

I love animals. I told Jack when we married that I slept with my little dog, and he was welcome to join us. My heart cheers up whenever I see squirrels and chipmunks in my backyard or a cardinal couple at my birdfeeder. I delighted in California this past week watching lizards scurry around the grounds of the retreat center. I have always had an extremely close relationship with my own pets, and a delight in all God's creatures. But, my love for animals goes deeper than just mere sentimentality. I hold a deep theological conviction the God is the Creator of all things. I believe that God, our Creator, has given humankind the responsibility to care for His creation. I believe that Jesus Christ is Lord of all creation, and therefore humans, animals, and plants, the whole earth, belongs to Him. "The earth is the Lord's," the Psalmist declares, "and all that is in it." (Psalm 24:1). All creatures were created by God, the animals of the forest, the birds of the air, all the sea creatures, the lions, the creeping things, all living things both great and small were created by God to whom they all look for their care (Psalm 104:17-30) Therefore, we as humans have no absolute rights over lower creations. We have the duty to look after them as God would look after them. We have the responsibility, as those given dominion over the earth, to exercise great care and protection for all created things. We are to honor all life for the sake of the Lord who gave them life.

It is extremely clear in Scripture that God loves, kindly cares for, and delights in his animal creations. After making them, God pronounced, "This is good." In Genesis 9, God made a covenant after the flood not just with Noah, but with all the animals too. When God speaks to Job he goes on and on about the wonder and grandeur of the things he has created, especially proud of wild animals like lions, mountain goats, oxen, ostriches, horses, hawks and whales (Job 38-41). God lamented at the end of the book of Jonah over the possible destruction of Nineveh's animals, who would have been innocently included if the whole city had been destroyed (Jonah 4:11). Jesus reminds us that even the tiny sparrows are not forgotten by God. "Not one of them will fall to the ground apart from your Father," Jesus promises.

Throughout the Old Testament, God uses animals in his great plan for Israel. Today's amazing story is just one instance when God uses his animal creatures to help the human creatures. First, God uses **animals as a means of God's protection of us**. Balaam was too blind to see the angel with a drawn sword. His donkey turned off the road to avoid the angel, and was beaten for it. The donkey avoided the angel a second time in the narrow path, but crushed Balaam's foot in the process. Again, Balaam beat the donkey. When the donkey approached the angel a third time and saw no way around, he lay down. Enduring a third beating, God gives the donkey language. Balaam later finds out that if the donkey had not avoided the angel, Balaam would have died. The donkey protected the human.

There is a story from Thailand, that right before the tsunami on December 26, 2004, elephants sensed the danger and fled to higher ground, some with riders on their backs who were spared drowning because of the elephants' flight. National Geographic Magazine reports that the day the tsunami hit dogs refused to go outdoors, zoo animals retreated far inside their shelters and could not be enticed to come out, and flamingos abandoned low lying areas. Along India's coast, where thousands of people perished, the Indo-Asian News service reported that buffaloes, goats, and dogs were found unharmed. Very few animals were found dead. Wildlife experts believe animals' more acute hearing and other senses might enable them to hear or feel the Earth's vibration, tipping them off to approaching disaster long before humans realize what's going on.[17] What if humans had been smart enough to closely watch and take a clue from the animals that something was about to happen? Another story which made national news and appeared in Guideposts magazine was about a man whose car had gone off the road and fallen into a ravine. He was saved by the dog with him who went to get help. Animals are used by God to protect us in amazing ways.

Secondly, **animals are a means of God's provision for us.** Animals provide food for us, most with the gift of their lives. Animals provide clothing for us. Have you noticed that the first animal death occurred after and as a result of the fall of humanity? God, as Adam and Eve were kicked out of the garden, knew they needed something to wear in the harsh environment into which he was about to send them besides those ridiculous fig leaf garments they had sewn for themselves. So, God made garments of animal skin for the humans and clothed them properly.

Animals provide transportation for us. Balaam's donkey makes a great point in the discussion with Balaam: "Aren't I your own donkey, which you have always ridden? Have I been in the habit of doing this?" No, the donkey had not been in the habit. Balaam's donkey had faithfully been his beast of burden. Sometimes I think about the awesome responsibility of the donkey that carried Mary to Bethlehem for the birth of Jesus, and the donkey that carried Jesus triumphantly into Jerusalem. What an important role in the plan and

---

[17] Maryann Mott, *National Geographic News*, January 4, 2005.

purpose of God they had!

Animals provide companionship for us. Their companionship is deep and lasting. It is unconditionally loving. It is an example of the presence of God in our lives. There are so many people for whom the presence and care of an animal is crucial, and for whom the loss of such a companion is extremely difficult.

When I was pregnant with Taylor, I was extremely anxious. I had miscarried twice before. My father called one day to say a stray Yorkshire terrier had been found outside his office and asked if I could take it in until the owner was found. I said, "Sure!" and spent the day with the little dog putting up signs. I spent the next day with the little dog taking down all the signs I had put up. Sandee was staying with me. And for nine months, she never left my side. When my belly got big enough, Sandee would sit on top. With Sandee beside me, my anxiety left. I can't explain it except to say her companionship was a tangible sign of the presence of God, who is with me always.

And lastly, **animals are a means of God's grace to us.** The lions closed their mouths while Daniel was in their den, much to the surprise of King Darius. The whale swallowed Jonah to keep him from drowning. The animals kept Mary, Joseph, and baby Jesus warm the night he was born. Balaam's donkey took beatings to spare him. Dogs, monkeys, and other animals work to help many who are paralyzed, blind, or ill with diseases like epilepsy. Animals bring healing joy to children with cancer. So much grace, healing, and goodness from God comes to us through animals.

Jama Hedgecoth, founder and director of Noah's Ark, a rehabilitation facility that brings animals and abused children together, watched 10-year-old Sarah sitting by herself under an oak tree, far from the other kids playing kickball in the Georgia sun.

Since Sarah arrived at their foster home a week earlier, she hadn't said a word to Jama, or her husband Charlie, or to the other kids. Nor had she wanted to play with any of the displaced animals at Noah's Ark Animal Rehabilitation Center.

"She's been abused from a young age," the social worker had warned them. "No one's been able to help her." "I'll be able to," Jama thought. But whenever she went to hug Sarah she stood as stiff as a pole, arms clamped to her sides. The night Sarah came to Noah's Ark, she barely ate a bite of her dinner. Jama asked her over and over, "Honey, what can I do for you?" Sarah just gave a blank stare. A couple of nights later she and Charlie passed by her room and heard sobbing. Jama knocked and went in. Sarah hushed, but she could see her body trembling. Back in the hallway she whispered to Charlie, "How do we reach Sarah?" Charlie responded, "Maybe we just need to wait."

One afternoon as she watched Sarah pick listlessly at a tuft of grass, she was about to ask for the thousandth time, "Honey, why are you hurting?" Then she spied one of their fawns. It wobbled close to Sarah, who looked up for a second, then dropped her head. Jama drew in her breath as the fawn climbed onto Sarah's lap. Then the fawn licked Sarah's face with its velvety tongue. She started to rush over to tell her that it was okay. *Wait, Jama.* The words came loud and clear in her mind. She knew the message came from God. "But she's scared," she thought. *Just wait*, God told her again.

The fawn kept licking Sarah's cheeks, dodging her efforts to push it away. At last Sarah stopped struggling. She slowly moved her hands across the fawn's speckled back. And then Sarah was hugging the fawn as it licked her tears away. That night Sarah spoke to Jama and Charlie for the first time. Soon she was playing kickball with the other kids and helping feed the animals, including the little fawn.[18] God's grace came through an animal, when it could come no other way.

Isaiah had a vision (Isaiah 65:17-25). He saw a new heaven and a new earth where wolves and lambs live together in peace, where lions eat straw like the ox, and where humans' days will be long and blessed, dwelling in the midst of the Lord their God. On God's holy mountain, nothing, neither humans or animals, will be hurt or destroyed. Isaiah understood like Paul in Romans 8, that all creation is groaning and waiting for the day when Jesus comes back and brings Isaiah's vision to reality.

I believe the people of God must live into Isaiah's vision and must imitate God's love and care for all creation, including the animals. Every year, billions of God's creatures experience automated, institutionalized, routine, and often cruel destruction for food, for profit, for science, and for sport. This should bother Christians greatly, for as Andrew Linzey put it, "to stand with Jesus is to stand for God's justice and the final release of all creation from bondage to decay."[19] To stand with Jesus means to stand with and care for all he has created and will ultimately redeem.

There are many ways we can do this. We can care for our own pets well. We can help those animals who are harmed or discarded by others. We can boycott products and organizations that do needless harm to animals, such as the March of Dimes, which subjects animals to horrific torture. And we can thank the Lord for the protection, provision, and grace that his wonderful creatures have brought into our lives.

---

[18] Jama Hedgecoth, *Jama's Ark*, printed in Guideposts and on Noah's Ark website
[19] Andrew Linzey, *Animal Gospel* (Louisville: Westminster John Knox Press, 2000), 15.

What Complaining Can Do

Numbers 14:1-35; Philippians 2:14-15

Jim Cymbala, pastor of the Brooklyn Tabernacle in Brooklyn, New York, was welcoming new members after a worship service when he said something he had not planned on saying to them. He said, prompted by the Holy Spirit he believes, "And now I charge you as members of this church that if you ever hear another member speak an unkind word of criticism, complaint, or slander against anyone – myself, an usher, a choir member, or anyone else – that you stop that member in mid-sentence and say, "Excuse me – who hurt you? Who ignored you? Who slighted you? Was it Pastor Cymbala? Let's go to his office right now. He will apologize to you and then we'll pray together so God can restore peace to this body. But we won't let you talk critically about people who aren't present to defend themselves." "I'm serious about this," he says, "and to this day every time we receive new members, I say much the same thing. That's because I know what most easily destroys churches. It's not crack cocaine or government oppression, or even lack of funds. Rather it's gossip, slander, [and complaining] that grieves the Holy Spirit."[20]

Yes, today's sermon is about complaining. This sermon is for me just as much as it is for you. If you know anything about Myers-Briggs personality testing, I am a strong J, a judger. I quickly decide what I like and don't like. I see flaws easily. On top of that, I am a perfectionist, and my personality is very predisposed to complaint and criticism when something is not perfect. The one good thing about my personality is that I am much harder on myself than I am

---

[20] Jim Cymbala, *Fresh Wind, Fresh Fire: What Happens When God's Spirit Invades the Hearts of His People* (Grand Rapids: Zondervan, 1997).

on others. But I have a right to my opinion, don't I? I feel better when I have the chance to express it. And complaining about something wrong sometimes makes it right. But there are other amazing things complaining can do. Think with me today about what complaining does in our Bible readings for today.

Complaining blinds us to the blessings God has given us. The Hebrew people had been freed by God from harsh slavery in the land of Egypt. They had miraculously avoided the awful plagues God sent upon Egypt, passed through the Red Sea on dry land, and witnessed the destruction of the Egyptian army after them. God led them with a cloud by day and fire by night. God provided ample food in the wilderness: manna and quail for the people to eat and water for them to drink. They are at the edge of the Promised Land. Spies have just returned from that land and reported that it is a land flowing with milk and honey and with unusually large fruit. But the spies also reported that the people who live there are strong and their cities are fortified. Caleb and Joshua, two of the twelve, were optimistic and testified that God could give them this land. The other ten were pessimistic and said, "We cannot go up against these people."

This is where we pick up our story today. When the people heard the report of the ten, they complained. "It would have been better to stay in Egypt. Why did you bring us out here to die? Now we will be killed by the sword and our wives and children taken." "Let's get rid of Moses and Aaron," they decided. They even came close to stoning Joshua and Caleb when they encouraged the people again to trust in the Lord.

Why? Why did they do this? Had they forgotten all God had promised them? Had they forgotten all that God had done in the past, the miracles witnessed with their own eyes? Did they prefer slavery over freedom? No, they were just complainers. And their complaining blinded them to what they already had. Complaining can easily become a habit, an addiction even, not just in ancient times, but today too. *Workforce Magazine* noticed it in workers before the recession. "It's a lot like a mathematics equation gone horribly wrong. Hmm - let's see: they had the lowest unemployment in decades, companies scrambling to woo new workers, more money than ever spent on workplace programs. These factors should all add up to a satisfied work force. Not so. Instead, companies nationwide reported quite the opposite.

"Ronald M. Katz, assistant vice president of corporate employee relations at Chase Manhattan Bank, is continually surprised by the increase in his employees' complaints. "Now, this wasn't a rough-and-tumble industry we're talking about. This was banking, [before the crisis]. And it's not just any bank, but the well-respected Chase Manhattan Bank - a perennial favorite for lists like Working Mothers' list of 'Best Companies for Working Mothers,' and an organization lauded for employee programs from flexible work arrangements to diversity initiatives."[21]   Why did so few workers realize how good they had it?

The same is true in the church today. So, few members realize how blessed we are to worship in freedom, to worship in a sanctuary, to know the love and power of God, and to have Christian friends to help and support us. Instead we complain about everything, big or small. We complain about things like paint color, carpet color, doing repairs, not doing repairs, not being asked to help, being asked to help, the church changing too much, the church changing too little, the sanctuary being too cold, the sanctuary being too hot, not having enough, buying too much, worship being too long, too traditional,

---

[21] Gillian Flynn, "Why Employees Are So Angry," *Workforce*, September 1998, 27

too contemporary, and the list goes on and on. The complaining blinds us to the blessings we already have and the amazing things God is doing in us and with us.

Complaining hurts our witness as Christians. Paul wrote the Philippians telling them to do everything without complaining or arguing, so that they could become blameless and pure, shining like stars in the world. The converse is true. If we complain and grumble and argue, we will not shine like stars. We will keep the world away. Who wants to join an organization that is unhappy and disgruntled? Not me. Our complaining betrays the fact that we have been given so much love, so much grace, and so much mercy from God. Complaining is a very poor witness to the Lord.

God is so upset at the complaining of the Hebrews that he tells Moses he would like to send a pestilence upon them and disinherit them. God will start again with Moses and make a great nation. But Moses argues a good point to God. He says, "Look how bad this will look to other nations. They will hear about it. They will talk about how the Lord was not able to bring them into the Promised Land." In others words, Moses argues that it will be a bad witness for God. God responds to Moses' argument, and relents from destroying them.

The world is watching the people of God. God's reputation can suffer because of what we do. Complaining destroys our ability to testify to the power and goodness of the Lord.

Complaining causes us to miss the good things God has planned for us in the future. God is so disappointed by the complaining of his people that he causes them to wander in the desert for 40 more years, so that those who complained would die before reaching the Promised Land. Their complaints (on at least ten different occasions) made them miss the wonderful land given to them, miss sharing it with their children, miss all the blessings of God that were to come if they had just been thankful and obedient. Complaining not only keeps us from good things externally, but keeps us from becoming in our hearts and minds who God who have us be. If we complain about every inconvenience, every issue that does not go our way, we will not learn from the hard times or grow stronger from our testing. But if we can keep ourselves from complaining, keep ourselves obedient and thankful, we know that our future is bright because our future is with God. "No eye has seen, nor ear has heard, nor heart conceived what God has prepared for those who love him," (1 Corinthians 2:9). Complainers will miss it.

It is told that the great concert violinist Niccolo Paganini was playing with a full orchestra in front of a packed house. He was playing several very difficult pieces including his favorite violin concerto. Shortly after he began the piece, one of the strings on his violin snapped and hung down from the instrument. Relying on his genius, he improvised and played on the next three strings. To his awful surprise a second string broke. He played the piece on the two remaining strings until you guessed it, a third string snapped. He finished the piece on one string. The audience leapt to their feet and applauded until their hands were numb. They never thought to ask for an encore; they expected to leave. But Paganini held his instrument high in the air and said, "Paganini and one string," and he proceeded to play an encore with the full orchestra. He made more music from that one string than many violinists ever could with four.

The difference was not only his incredible talent, but was his attitude. Instead of falling into despair and self-pity, complaining about the poor quality of strings these days, Paganini's splendid attitude allowed him to take a very difficult situation and turn it into a triumph.

Everyone has strings break at one time or another. Sometimes two, even three at one time. Complaining seems the thing to do in those times. There is always something to complain about, especially in the church. We are not perfect and never will be. As we have seen today, complaining is a very powerful activity. It can blind us to blessings we have, ruin our witness in the world, and block us from our future. Is complaining worth all that?

My answer is no; it is not. And with all the strength I can muster, I vow not to complain. I will remember the goodness and power of the Lord and play with the strings I am given. I have purple wristbands for everyone as a reminder. Make sure and get one from the ushers as you leave. Leave it on your wrist for 21 days. Every time you complain, switch it to the other wrist and start your 21 days over again. If we can go 21 days without complaining, we can go 365. O my friends, if our church can learn to do this, we will shine like stars in the heavens and we will find ourselves in the Promised Land at the end.

Even His Greatest Enemy

Acts 9:1-20

Jesus was crucified, dead and buried. On the third day, he rose again and appeared to the women, to the disciples, and to over five hundred witnesses before he ascended into heaven. More and more people were added to the number of believers in Jesus daily. The religious leaders were getting anxious, determined to stamp out this new movement. Those who were followers of The Way (the earliest name for those who believed) were being arrested, persecuted, even killed.

Stephen, one of the first deacons of the church, was called before the council, and as those before him had done, he proclaimed before them that Jesus is the Messiah and that they had killed him, but God raised him from the dead. The Council could take no more. They gnashed their teeth and covered their ears. They rushed Stephen, dragged him out of the city and stoned him to death.

Saul, a young Pharisee gaining power, held the coats of those stoning Stephen and he approved of it. Saul then led a severe persecution of Christians in Jerusalem, entering house after house, dragging men and women of The Way off to prison. The others fled Jerusalem for the countryside and surrounding countries.

While this story in Acts, the story of Saul's conversion, tells us much about Saul and the opposition to the early church, it tells us more about Jesus. The main character in every conversion story is Jesus. It is Jesus who changes lives. So, let's look at what this story of conversion tells us about Jesus.

Even His Greatest Enemy is loved and sought. Saul's story is the second of three dramatic conversion stories told in this part of Acts.

Philip tells an Ethiopian official about Jesus, and he is baptized. Peter is sent to the home of Cornelius, a Roman centurion, who believes, as do all those gathered in his home to hear Peter speak, and they all receive – Gentiles receive – the gift of the Holy Spirit. Two very unexpected outsiders were loved and sought out by Jesus through his earliest disciples.

In Saul's case, Saul was not an outsider. He was an insider: a Jew and a religious leader. And yet, he was Jesus' greatest enemy at that time. He was violently persecuting the church and trying to destroy it. He was more zealous in this than any other Jewish leader.

Why would Jesus seek out his enemy? Wasn't it Jesus who said, "Love your enemies and pray for those who persecute you, so that you may be children of your Father in heaven . . . If you love those who love you, what reward do you have?" Wasn't it Jesus who described the kingdom of God like a shepherd searching for a lost sheep, a woman desperately searching for a lost coin, and a father waiting and running toward a lost son? Jesus is just doing what he taught, what is consistent with his character. He loves and searches for even those who hate him.

Jesus loved Saul, his number one enemy. Jesus sought him out, finding a way to reach him. Jesus seeks everyone out, looking for an opening, waiting for a turn, ready to jump into action at the right moment. Pray for those who are enemies of Jesus, or who don't know him. Jesus loves and seeks us all.

Even His Greatest Enemy is won with his loving presence. Do you remember the hit movie, *Three Men and a Baby*? It's a wonderful story of three men who have their lives pretty well under control. They are talented, popular, and rich. Suddenly, their whole world is turned upside down by the presence of a baby. That gentle presence among them reordered their priorities, challenged their vocations, and taught them a new way to live. It also filled their home with love. It's the same with Jesus. Once we encounter his loving, powerful presence in our own lives, then our world is turned upside down, our priorities are reordered, and we learn a new way to live our lives. That's why conversion is often called being, "born again."

Paul is on the road to Damascus when he is confronted with the powerful but loving presence of Jesus. Jesus says to him, "Saul, Saul, why are you persecuting me?" Jesus calls him by name. Jesus doesn't condemn him. Jesus doesn't humiliate him. Jesus doesn't hurt him. He confronts him with himself. "I am Jesus, the one you are hell bent on denying. Wake up! Get with it! I'm here! I'm real!"

Not everyone is an enemy of Jesus like Saul was. Many are not breathing threats and murder, but may be doing injury to themselves and those around them, relentlessly pursuing something against the kingdom of God. Maybe some are so determined to get a promotion they risk losing their marriage; maybe so locked up emotionally that they can't express love to their spouse; maybe a sports enthusiast incapable of seeing there are things more important than games; maybe parenting in a way that is so hard and demanding that that child can never get a break; maybe hanging on to some old prejudice, some tradition, some habit that holds Jesus back   all good reasons for conversion. Whatever the reason may be, conversions happen all the time and need to happen all the time.

Not everyone has a "Damascus Road" experience like Paul. We don't see a blinding light or hear the actual voice of Jesus. But we do experience his presence. Some describe it as an overwhelming sense of peace. Some hear a word of truth and tingle inside. Some describe the love of God in Jesus Christ tearing down walls around them. But, there's not one religious experience that fits everybody. Pray for those who are seeking and searching, that they will hear and see

Jesus. Pray God will open all our eyes to the new reality created by his life, death and resurrection. We are all won by his loving presence.

Even His Greatest Enemy is wanted for service. Being loved, sought, and won is not the end. Christianity is not just about conversion; it is about vocation. We are all instruments to be used by God for his glory. We are ambassadors for Christ, partners with God in the reconciliation of the world. We have gifts and a calling from God to use them for his kingdom.

Saul becomes Paul. Paul's mission is to carry the gospel to the Gentile world. His passion, instead of working against Jesus, now works for him. He spreads the gospel throughout the known world with his travels, his speeches and his letters. In less than 300 years, Christianity will become the official religion of the Roman Empire.

Francis Collins, a physician and physicist, head of the Human Genome Project, describes himself as a once "obnoxious atheist." "I became an atheist," he states, "because as a graduate student studying quantum physics, life seemed to be reducible to second-order differential equations. Mathematics, chemistry and physics had it all. And I didn't see any need to go beyond that. Frankly, I was at a point in my young life where it was convenient for me to not have to deal with a God. I kind of liked being in charge myself. But then I went to medical school, and I watched people who were suffering from terrible diseases. And one of my patients, after telling me about her faith and how it supported her through her terrible heart pain, turned to me and said, 'What about you? What do you believe?' And I stuttered and stammered and felt the color rise in my face, and said, 'Well, I don't think I believe in anything.' But it suddenly seemed like a very thin answer. And that was unsettling. I was a scientist who was supposed to draw conclusions from the evidence and I realized at that moment that I'd never really looked at the evidence for and against the possibility of God."

So, he did look for evidence and after reading the book *Mere Christianity* by C.S. Lewis (another once atheist scholar) he became a believer in Jesus. God now uses him in the scientific community, a place that sorely needs advocates for God, to argue that science and faith are not incompatible. This puts Collins in an awkward position sometimes, for most of his colleagues think he is crazy for believing in Jesus, and yet they cannot deny his scientific excellence. He discovered the gene that causes cystic fibrosis.[22]

So, if we have been loved and sought and won by Jesus, it is so that we can be used by him. We may not change the world, we may not be martyred, but we will have an important role as followers of The Way. We may never know until we get to the other side what we accomplished for Jesus by the little acts of faithfulness we did. Pray for all those using their gifts to work against Jesus. Pray they will be transformed.

And so my friends, I ask you. What kind of God can turn even his greatest enemy into his most ardent supporter? An awesome, amazing, loving, saving, healing, powerful, creative and calling God, made know to us in Jesus Christ. That's a God worth believing in!

---

[22] www.salon.com/books/int/2006/08/07/collins/

Destiny

Ephesians 1:3-14

It starts at an airport baggage claim area. Two identical bags appear on the carousel. A man grabs the one he thinks is his and heads home. He opens it to unpack later that evening and finds not his clothes but a woman's: lingerie, hose, high heel shoes, blouses, skirts, a few souvenirs from San Francisco. He notices the faint, sweet smell of perfume. He looks at the tag and sees the name and address of this woman. She lives on the other side of town. He calls her and apologizes for any inconvenience he may have caused her and offers to bring the bag to her house. She is thankful to have found her bag and gives him directions. When he arrives and she opens the door, they are both pleasantly surprised. They are attracted to each other. They soon find out they are both single and decide to have dinner. One thing leads to another and six months later they are married. Friends and family proclaim it was destiny that brought them together. It was destiny that he picked up her bag by mistake. It was in the stars.

We often think of destiny this way, associating it with Ouija boards, crystal balls, and astrology. Sometimes, we see destiny as having little to do with, if not the opposite of, God. Destiny is thought of as an impersonal force beyond our control. However, Christians believe strongly in destiny, God's destiny for our lives. Presbyterians especially cling to a doctrine called predestination, the idea that God has a destiny in mind for all of us. We have taken a lot of heat for this doctrine of destiny because it has been used for unloving purposes and misunderstood. The doctrine of predestination does not claim that everything that happens to us is predetermined and is God's will for our lives. If it rains on our wedding day or if we cannot find a parking place, if we find or lose a job, if a loved one becomes ill and recovers or dies, it would be wrong to see these happy or tragic events as God's pre-determined plan for our lives. "Whatever will be, will be" is not predestination.

Predestination is a Biblical doctrine that has specifically to do with what God has destined us to and for in this life and the next. What is our calling? What is God's plan for our life here and in eternity? What is our destiny? We find it in the Old Testament, in the story of Abraham. God chose Abraham and destined him to be a great nation and a blessing to all the families of the earth. We find it in the call of Jeremiah. The Lord said to him, "Before I formed you in the womb I knew you, and before you were born I consecrated you." The Lord speaks through Jeremiah to the people of Israel saying, "Surely I know the plans I have for you, plans for good and not for evil, to give you a future with hope." We see it in Jesus' words to his disciples, "You did not choose me but I chose you."

Our text from Ephesians speaks of us being destined for adoption as God's children. We are chosen by God to be members of his own family, chosen from before the beginning of time. That's why we say pre-destination. It was before we were ever born, before we had the chance to do well with our lives or to mess them up. God chose that we should be his, no matter what.

In the time that Ephesians was written, adoption was common. Adopted children were given all the rights of natural born children with one additional guarantee. In the ancient world, adopted children could not be disowned for any reason. They were a permanent member of the family. God's choice, before the foundation of the world, was to adopt us, to love us and provide for us. It is our destiny to be adopted as God's children, and receive the inheritance of the children of God. This inheritance includes redemption and forgiveness of sins through Jesus Christ and it is wonderful and impossible to imagine what else awaits us. The highest experiences of peace and joy in this world are only faint foretastes of what God has prepared for us.

Why as believers is it important to know our destiny? The doctrine of destiny is, first, an assurance for us. It is assurance that our lives are in God's hands rather than in the grasp of an impersonal fate or under the control of an astrological sign. We are not on pre-set courses based on our DNA, for better or for worse. Our future is certain with God.

The doctrine of destiny assures us that we have value. There are no "accidents" from a night of passion. God has a plan, a purpose, a destiny for all human life. God chose each person before the foundation of the world.

Predestination is an assurance that stands over and against any works righteousness. It opposes every effort of ours to earn our salvation. God chose and destined us to be his holy and blameless children, doing for us through Jesus Christ, what we could not do for ourselves.

Some people look for assurance in the external condition of their lives. They interpret sickness, trouble and tragedy as signs that God is against them; comfort, prosperity, and success as signs that God is on their side. This certainly isn't true for God's people. Take for example John the Baptist. There is no doubt that he had been chosen by God for a wonderful task: to be the preparation for the Messiah. There is no doubt of John's destiny. Yet he sat in prison and lost his head at the whim of an evil person and as the result of a prideful and drunken promise. Christians are not people who are sure God is on their side if they escape hardship or distress. They are people who know that God is with them and for them in the midst of the worst that can happen. For nothing will be able to separate us from the love of God in Christ Jesus our Lord.

If the doctrine of destiny is an assurance, it is also a challenge. It challenges us to live out that to which we have been called. We are destined so that we can be the instruments of God to bring blessing to others. God chose Abraham in order to bless all the earth. And so, it is with us. We are chosen, destined, not instead of but for the sake of the outsider, for the sake of those who don't know or have rejected their destiny. We are destined not to escape from a godless world, but are sent into it to live for it.

Because we are now adopted children of God, we take on the characteristics of the family. We let our light shine, we care for the widow and the orphan and the stranger, we work for justice and peace, we serve Christ's church joyfully, we love one another as we have been loved. We have the responsibility to invite others into the family, their destiny as well.

Many of you know that my daughter Alia spent the first three and a half years of her life in an orphanage in northern Kazakhstan. We found out that she would join our family in October of 2000, but could not travel to get her until April, 2001. During the six months, we waited before going to get Alia in Kazakhstan, the Kazaks experienced their worst winter in over fifty years. They had massive amounts of snow and many nights, the temperature descended to -40°C. I wondered if she was warm. I wondered if she had enough to eat. I wondered if she had enough to wear. I wondered if she had someone to love her and kiss her goodnight. But most of all, I wondered if she knew that halfway around the world three people loved her like one of their own and couldn't wait to bring her into their family. How does God see those he loves but who don't know he exists? Is God more passionate about them than I was about Alia? You bet God is!

Did Alia know what awaited her? She couldn't image a room of her own, a house without locked doors, a pantry full of snacks, swimming pools, flush toilets, toys of her very own. There's no way she knew that in America, the world was hers, if she chose to take it. How could a three-year-old know that her destiny was love and family in world she did not even know existed? How can those who are apart from God's family know what awaits them? Can they know that someone who seems so far away loves them and wants to bring them into the family? They cannot even imagine it.

Someone must have prepared Alia and told her we were on our way, for the first instant we saw her, she held up her arms and said, "Mama". I bent down and she grabbed my cheeks and kissed me Russian style – one peck on each cheek.

What can we do to prepare someone to meet God, hold up their arms, and cry, "Abba"? What can we tell them about our family that makes then grab their destiny with both hands and kiss it? Do we know ourselves as God's adopted children, loved and secure? Are we living out both the pleasures and the responsibilities of being chosen in Jesus Christ? I hope so. It's our destiny.

Don't Panic!

Acts 16:16-34

I have what is supposed to be an excerpt from the U.S. Government Peace Corps Manual for those who work in the Amazon jungle instructing them in what to do in case one is attacked by an anaconda. Listen closely. Who knows when any of us may be attacked by an anaconda?

"If you are attacked by an anaconda, do not run. The snake is faster than you are. Lie flat on the ground. Put your arms tight against your sides, your legs tight against one another. Tuck your chin in. The snake will come and begin to nudge and climb over your body. Do not panic. After the snake has examined you, it will begin to swallow you from the feet end – always from the feet end. Permit the snake to swallow your feet and ankles. Do not panic. The snake will now begin to suck your legs into its body. You must lie perfectly still. This will take a long time. Do not panic. When the snake has reached your knees, slowly, and with as little movement as possible, reach down, take your knife and very gently slide it into the side of the snake's mouth between the edge of its mouth and your leg. Then suddenly rip upward, severing the snake's head. Be sure you have your knife." I guess if you don't have your knife, then you can panic.

As unrealistic as the advice in the Peace Corps manual may be, its general premise is correct: Don't panic. Our reading from Acts today carries the same message for those who are of faith in Jesus Christ: No matter what your current situation may be, don't panic!

We see some good examples of panic in our text. The owners of a slave girl possessed by an evil spirit panic when Paul heals her and her fortune-telling powers are no more. Their source of income is gone. Her owners then convene a kangaroo court with the local authorities, angry that Paul and Silas have healed her. They have broken no laws, and yet are accused of disturbing the city. The owners play the race card, bringing up that Paul and Silas are Jews.

The mention of their Jewish ethnicity and the prejudice in the crowd's reaction causes the magistrates to panic. Without thinking, without bothering to find out if Paul and Silas are Roman citizens, which they are, the magistrates have them beaten severely and thrown into prison. When they try to let Paul and Silas go quietly later in chapter 16, Paul and Silas refuse, reminding them of the fact that they are citizens and were beaten and jailed illegally.

The jailer is the most panicked of all in this situation. An earthquake is scary enough, but the thought that his prisoners have escaped was too much to bear. He would be executed if his prisoners escaped. His panic over the situation drove him to a near suicide, until Paul intervened. Panic leads us to all kinds of immature actions and harmful emotions: anger, bitterness, fear, and despair.

Paul and Silas are the two in this story who do not panic. Falsely accused and arrested for doing something good, they are stripped and harshly beaten. They are thrown in jail, in the innermost cell, and put in stocks. Surely there is no escape at midnight from the cell where they are chained. So, what do they do? Do they vow revenge? Do they call their lawyer and complain? Do they cry or pout? Do they give up? Quit the evangelism circuit? Vow to never attend church again? Do they accuse God of not caring about them? No! They pray and sing hymns. They pray and sing hymns. Seems like a strange reaction to their situation. It seems not to fit. It seems to be the opposite of what two men should do whose lives are on the line.

So, what is the difference? Why do Paul and Silas refuse to panic? Why do the men, who are the ones who should be panicking, decide to, at midnight, communicate with God in word and song? It is because Paul and Silas believe in Jesus Christ. They believe what they told the jailer to be true: believe on the Lord Jesus Christ and you will be saved. Salvation certainly meant eternal life after death for Paul and Silas. But it also meant for them a peace and a confidence now that no beating, no prison, no opposition, not even death could separate them from the love of God in Jesus Christ their Lord.

While pain, illness, disappointment, and loss can work to separate us from other persons and from God, Paul and Silas knew that it is prayer that reconnects us with God. Prayer is not a denial of the harsh realities of life. Prayer puts everything in perspective, reminding us that we find our meaning and purpose in our Creator. Prayer reminds us that we are part of something much larger than our current situation. Prayer, both talking and listening to God, reminds us that God is still at work in our world, transforming our world – you may not see any of it on the nightly news, but it is happening.

Mogopa, a village to the west of Johannesburg, was to be demolished and its inhabitants forcibly removed at gunpoint in South African apartheid's forced population removal schemes. On the eve of their departure, a vigil with church leaders from all over South Africa was held in Mogopa. The village clinic, shops, schools and churches had already been demolished. At about midnight, an elder of the doomed village got up to pray, and he prayed a strange prayer that Bishop Desmond Tutu reports and will never forget. He prayed, "God, thank you for loving us so much."

Years later now, apartheid is dead and the people of Mogopa returned and rebuilt. God did indeed love them very much, it seems. I wonder what Paul and Silas prayed that night? I wonder if their prayers may have been as simple and confident as the people in Mogopa, "God, thank you for loving us so much."

Even those at their wits end, who have prayers long buried in their hearts and minds can receive the benefits of it. I will never forget talking with a certain patient at the state mental hospital in Austin, TX. She was schizophrenic and some of our conversations had absolutely no rooting in reality. I was never sure if she was able to process anything I said. The voices in her head were so loud and so horrible. So, one day, after a summer of what I perceived as failure as her chaplain, I gave up and just started praying the Lord's Prayer. I couldn't think of anything else to pray. About half way through, at "give us this day our daily bread" she joined in and with perfect memory and timing prayed the rest of the prayer with me. That prayer made the prison she was in a little brighter. That prayer opened a door that had long been closed by her illness. Never underestimate the power of prayer.

Paul and Silas also knew that it is the singing of our faith that cements it into our hearts and minds like nothing else. We are commanded in Scripture to sing. Among God's greatest gifts to us in times of turmoil are the great songs, both ancient and modern, that remind us of the truths of our faith. Every time we sing the great hymns and praise songs, we are proclaiming what we believe in a powerful and pervasive way. Christians always have something to sing about.

Paul and Silas did what exemplary believers of all time must do while waiting for God to act: praying and singing. Not panicking. Paul and Silas' lack of panic, and their subsequent prayers and songs did much more than just help the two of them. Our text says that all the prisoners were listening. When God did act on their behalf, and the earthquake came, none of the other prisoners panicked. They stayed right where they were. Their lack of panic caused the jailer to halt his suicide, and to inquire about and receive the gospel of Jesus Christ.

This is a truth that endures. The believers' reaction to difficult circumstances is a powerful witness to those around. When we react to hardship with faith, perseverance and hope, the non-believer is curious about what give us such confidence. When we react to difficulties with anger, bitterness, revenge, fear, or despair, the non-believer has no reason to want what we have been given. If anger, despair, complaining, and apathy have no place in a jail cell for the believer, then they certainly have no place in the church. Our help comes from the Lord who made heaven and earth. When we live and react like we believe it, others will notice and believe as well.

What if the boy you like doesn't know you exist? Don't panic. What if your company is laying off employees? Don't panic. What if you get a bad diagnosis from your doctor? Don't panic. What if your car breaks down? Don't panic. What if you are attacked by an anaconda? Don't panic. What if it seems like all hope is lost? Don't panic. Don't despair. Believe in Jesus Christ and his power and love for you.

Our victory comes not in the opening of stocks and doors, but in the stubborn refusal to panic. Our victory comes when we trust in the God of our salvation above all else. So, when things in our lives go from bad to worse, remember the story of Paul and Silas. Pray. Sing. And wait for the earthquake.

Passing on Judgment

Romans 14:1-12

Paul continues to describe how Christians who stand and fall on the grace of God in Christ Jesus our Lord must live. There are disagreements in the Roman Church, and from the reading it seems like there are disagreements over what to eat and what days are holy. Notice how Paul does not get involved in the actual issue or take a side. Surely Paul has an opinion – he's an opinionated guy. Instead he tells them not to despise those who see things differently and asks the very hard question: "Who are you to pass judgment on servants of another?" We are commanded not to pass judgment.

But does Paul mean we should never decide whether something is right or wrong? I don't think so. We must decide what is right and what is wrong, not just for ourselves, but for the church and our society in general. We must speak out against injustice and do what we can to alleviate suffering. We must make judgments all the time about what to do and what not to do. So what is Paul talking about?

I think by passing judgment he means deciding on the worth, the authenticity, and/or the faith of another Christian. I believe he means that ultimate judgment about someone is not ours to make. Society asks us to all the time. It is very tempting to do so. We should never do that, Paul argues, and there are very good reasons why instead of passing judgment, we must pass on judgment.

We must pass on judgment because our judgments are often wrong. I read a news story this week about a pair of brothers in prison for three decades for rape and murder. As it turns out, DNA evidence has cleared them. Three decades locked up because of an erroneous judgment.

The first month I was at a former call, the treasurer noticed on the bank statement that $3000 was missing from one of the accounts. She went to the bank and was told that a short woman with dark hair withdrew the money. She assumed it was me. She knew hiring a female pastor was bad idea. She talked to others about it. Finally, she and the finance elder came to confront me.

Of course, I knew nothing about it. If you know anything about the inner workings of the church, you know a pastor does not have access to any bank accounts. I have one pastor's discretionary fund from which I can draw funds to help in an emergency, but even for that fund I must submit a request with a valid bill and the check is still written by the bookkeeper and signed by the treasurer. I have no access to checks or withdrawal slips. It is a good system.

So, we all headed over to the bank. As it turns out, another short woman with dark hair (there must be a lot of us) who had an account at that bank had transposed the last two numbers of her account on her withdrawal slip, which was the number for the church's account. It was an innocent mistake by someone unknown to us, and the bank corrected it quickly.

What was not corrected so quickly was the judgment that had been made about me. Even though I had been cleared of any involvement, it had been talked about and you never know with those lady preachers. It took a long time to earn their trust and I must say it took me a long time to trust them. When we don't have all the information, and we rarely do, we make false judgments and they can be costly.

We must pass on judgment because we are imperfect. I hear a lot of Christians say, "Love the sinner, hate the sin." That is not in the Bible. What is in the Bible is what we heard Jesus ask in Matthew's gospel this morning: "Why do you see the speck in your neighbor's eye, but do not notice the log in your own eye? You hypocrite! First, take the log out of your own eye" (Matthew 7:1-5). Jesus says it another way in John's gospel: "Let anyone among you who is without sin cast the first stone" (John 8:7). He seems pretty serious about this. In fact, in that passage from Matthew, Jesus gives us a sobering warning: "Do not judge others, so that you may not be judged. For with the judgment you make you will be judged, and the measure you give will be the measure you get."

This scares me because our judgments are always so much harsher for others than for ourselves. Do you remember the story of David, when Nathan came to confront him about his sin with Bathsheba, another man's wife? Nathan tells David a story about a rich man with many flocks and herds who wanted the one little lamb owned by a poor man. A traveler came to the rich man and instead of preparing one of his own flock to feed the traveler, he took the poor man's one pet lamb. What should happen to this rich man, David? What is your judgment?

David's anger was greatly kindled against the man. He said to Nathan, "As the Lord lives, the man who has done this deserves to die; he shall restore the lamb fourfold, because he did this thing, because he had no pity" (2 Samuel 12:5). It is then that Nathan reveals to David: "You are the man!" Now that it is him, does he still think the man who did this deserves to die? We so easily get sucked into an angry mob mentality, calling for other people's heads, and find it so difficult to impose the same sentence on ourselves.

Finally, and most importantly, **we must pass on judgment because there is only one Judge capable of doing this job.** We have believed it since the very beginning of our faith and we proclaim it at least monthly with the Apostles' Creed: "I believe in God the Father Almighty, Maker of heaven and earth, and in Jesus

Christ His only Son our Lord, . . . who shall come to judge the living and the dead." Jesus is the one who has all the information, who knows the secrets of our minds and hearts, and who punishes in order to bring redemption. It is before Him we stand or fall, and he is able to make us stand. We are not accountable for what anyone else does. We are accountable to God for what we do. Maybe Christians should stop condemning others and worry about ourselves more.

Why am I wearing a Chris Davis jersey, after he failed two drug tests? Because I too have broken the rules of the PC (USA), the state of Maryland, and the District of Columbia, the latter of which there is photographic evidence. Would I like to make a statement about Ray Rice? I would not. I am passing on judgment. But I would like to make a statement about myself: I have injured others, not with fists, but with words. I am very sorry for every time I have done so and I promise to try as hard as I can to do better, for the sake of myself, my church, the Christian faith, and the overwhelming grace of God in Jesus Christ our Lord.

This I Know

John 9:1-41

John's gospel is called the book of signs. The seven miracles in John are called signs by John because they point to who Jesus is, because they show us much needed information about Jesus. In today's story, Jesus spits on the ground, makes clay, and applies it to the man's eyes. Jesus sends the man to wash it off and when he does he can see. Jesus healed many people without touching them and even without being in the same physical location with them. But in this story, our minds are propelled back to Genesis, when the Lord God formed humans from the dust of the ground. Jesus, by whom all things came into being, who knows our bodies better that we know them ourselves, used the ground again to heal by re-creating eyes that were broken.

The questions this miracle raises are most fascinating to me. It was understood in Jesus' culture that if one was handicapped or ill, it was because of sin. It was that person's fault, or the parents' fault. They thought this because it answered the most fundamental question about suffering. Surely it is someone's fault. "Why was this man blind in the first place?" the disciples ask. Why do people suffer?

Jesus' answer assures us that all infirmities are not because of sin. He assures us that this man was blind for a great purpose: so the glory of God might be revealed in him. Much like Beethoven's deafness without which he would not have quit performing and started composing so prolifically, without which we would not know his 5th or 9th symphonies, this man's blindness would lead to a great end.

We, like the disciples, have many questions about illness and physical handicaps. "Why?" is one of the most frequent questions people ask

God. Read the Psalms – they are full of "why?" questions. Volumes have been written on this topic and many solutions proposed, none satisfactory.

Many problems, even physical problems we have are the result of sin, of human error, or of bad habits. One of the liveliest members of the first church I served was little Sean*. Only three years old, Sean wandered into the garage at his grandparents' house and drank liquid Dursban, a potent pesticide. As he lay in the ICU unconscious and twitching from the effects of the poison, as I prayed over him, I knew why this happened. For only thirty seconds, someone didn't know where he was. For ten seconds, he used amazing fine motor skills to open the child-proof cap. For ten seconds, he drank what must have been a horrible tasting substance. Knowing why didn't help at all. Humans were at fault in this case. But as we gathered around his bed, as we laid our hands on him and prayed, something happened. Everyone in the room knew it. Something like an electric shock went through our hands and we all jumped. I can't explain how or why, but this I know: Sean survived with no lasting effects. He was near death and now he is alive.

Many times, there is no one to blame. Cancer comes uninvited into many lives. Accidents happen that could never have been foreseen. Children are stricken from birth with handicaps and conditions that are no one's fault. There is no theology to explain why: why some live and some die; why some respond to treatment and some don't; why some people are miraculously healed here on earth and some people must wait until death frees them from this frail body. We don't know why people suffer, but this we know: It is not always our fault and Jesus helps and heals those who are at fault and those who are not.

A second frequent question this miracle raises is this: Why do miracles happen? This is what the Pharisees are struggling so hard with in this story. How could Jesus heal him? He is a sinner. Only God can heal like that. The formerly blind man answers them so beautifully. "I don't know if he is a sinner or not. One thing I do know: I was blind and now I see."

My friend Jay, a United Methodist pastor, tells the story of when his best friend's wife got the news that she had cancer. She was a young woman with small children. The cancer was aggressive. He went to his place in the woods for serious prayer and he yelled at God for a long time. After his ranting and raving, words came clearly to his heart and mind: "Everything will be all right." "O sure," Jay said back to God. "What you mean by all right and what I mean by all right are two different things." He ranted and raved some more, questioning God's wisdom and fairness in this illness. When he finally had exhausted himself, the words filled his spirit again: "Everything will be all right." Everything was all right. After arduous treatment, she survived. Those children did not lose their mother prematurely. His friend did not lose his wife. I can't explain it. Many mothers do die early. Many do not survive cancer. But this I know: She was ill and now she's not. We don't know why miracles happen. But this I know: they do.

We don't have to explain it. We don't have to account for every case of illness and imperfection in human bodies. We will never know why and if we did it wouldn't help. We just witness to our own experience. "This I know," says the man born blind, "I was blind and now I see." Jesus healed him. He can't explain why he was chosen over the other thousands of blind people in Jerusalem. I can't explain why Lou, who showed such incredible strength and perseverance, was ravaged by cancer and ultimately lost the fight. I can't explain why a very sick baby's breathing improved dramatically after the church prayed for him and he was able to return home from the hospital. But this I know: Jesus is the Great Physician. Not only can he heal, he can also use any weakness, any infirmity, any handicap, whether he heals it now or in the life to come, to the glory of God. I don't know why miracles happen but this I know: To whom else would I take the sick and suffering?

A third question this miracle raises is this: Why are there so many who doubt, who refuse to believe who Jesus is? The Pharisees grill this man and his parents relentlessly wanting to prove the healing false. They question his true identity. They eventually kick him out of the synagogue. How ironic! The Pharisees had so much blinding them to who Jesus was: legalism, pride, ignorance, and an unwillingness to learn. Those attitudes cause us all to see and hear what we want to hear and to resist any change, anything that doesn't fit into our current theology or philosophy. The blindness of the Pharisees is much harder to heal that any physical blindness.

A story is told of a Presbyterian pastor who had a vision one afternoon while grilling steaks in his backyard. It changed his life. He shared his vision with the Session. Instead of rejoicing at his new spiritual insights, the church leaders offered to provide psychiatric care and paid administrative leave. This is the problem the man born blind encountered when he was healed. His new insight into who Jesus was and what he could do would turn the religious world of his day upside down.

I don't know why so many people don't believe, despite the overwhelming evidence that I see. I don't know why there will always be those who doubt and try to argue away Jesus' healing. But this I know: Jesus is the Son of Man, the Great Physician, the Savior of the world. Jesus shows us the incredible, amazing, healing love of

God in the flesh, again and again, eyewitness account after eyewitness account.

Jesus never explains the why. The question isn't "why" for Jesus. The question is always "Who?" The question is not "Who is at fault?" but "Who can do something about it?" He can. He is the one who comes upon one born blind from birth. Never since the world began has it been heard that anyone opened the eyes of a person born blind. But more importantly, who can open our spiritual eyes to see what God is up to in our world? This I know, because it has happened to me. Jesus can. Who can heal our bodies, minds, spirits, relationships, and churches? This I know because it happened to me, through me, and all around me. Jesus can. Who can take a life, with all its imperfections, and use it for his kingdom to the glory of God? This I know because it happened to me. Jesus can. The Lord is my shepherd; I shall not want. This I know, because I have experienced it myself. Surely goodness and mercy shall follow me all the days of my life, and I will dwell in the house of the Lord forever. This I know.

Let your knowledge of Jesus allow you to trust him in sickness and in health. Let your experience with him compel you to pray diligently for healing for family, friends, and co-workers, for all the sick people you know. Pray for all those who doubt. Set your faith high. Don't give in to the skeptics and doubters if you were blind and now you see. So what if you get kicked out of something? Believe, so that God's glory might be revealed in you. God will be glorified, even today in our skeptical world, by his healing mercy and love. This I know.

*This name has been changed.

About the Author

Rev. Dr. Tracey Davenport calls Texas home. She attended Baylor and George Mason Universities where she received a BS in Nursing. She worked at Baylor University Medical Center in Dallas, TX serving as a nurse in the liver and kidney transplant unit.

Tracey then attended Austin Presbyterian Theological Seminary. Following graduation and ordination, Tracey has served congregations in San Angelo, Texas and Stockbridge, Georgia. She currently serves as Senior Pastor/Head of Staff at Harundale Presbyterian Church in Glen Burnie, Maryland.

In 2012, Tracey received a Doctor of Ministry degree from Austin Presbyterian Theological Seminary with a focus of study in preaching Christian resistance to evil.

Tracey is married to Jack and they have two daughters and one dog. They love to watch sports and movies and travel together.

www.ingramcontent.com/pod-product-compliance
Lightning Source LLC
Chambersburg PA
CBHW071017120626
46546CB00003B/1129